RATTLER
ONE-SEVEN

A Vietnam Helicopter Pilot's War Story

CHUCK GROSS

Number 1 in the North Texas Military Biography and Memoir Series

University of North Texas Press
Denton, Texas

Printed in the United States of America.

10 9 8 7 6 5 4 3 2

Permissions:
University of North Texas Press
P.O. Box 311336
Denton, TX 76203-1336

The paper used in this book meets the minimum requirements of the American National Standard for Permanence of Paper for Printed Library Materials, z39.48.1984. Binding materials have been chosen for durability.

Library of Congress Cataloging-in-Publication Data

Gross, Chuck, 1950-
Rattler one-seven : a Vietnam helicopter pilot's war story / Chuck Gross.
p. cm. — (North Texas military biography and memoir series ; no. 1)
Includes bibliographical references and index.
ISBN-10: 1-57441-178-0 (cloth: alk. paper)
ISBN-13: 978-1-57441-178-2 (cloth: alk. paper)
ISBN-10: 1-57441-221-3 (paper: alk. paper)
ISBN-13: 978-1-57441-221-5 (paper: alk. paper)
1. Vietnamese Conflict, 1961-1975—Personal narratives, American. 2. Vietnamese Conflict, 1961-1975—Aerial operations, American. 3. Military helicopters—Vietnam. 4. Gross, Chuck, 1950- I. Title: Vietnam helicopter pilot's war story. II. Title. III. Series.
DS559.5.G76 2004
959.704'348'092—dc22

2004003457

Rattler One-Seven: A Vietnam Helicopter Pilot's War Story is Number 1 in the North Texas Military Biography and Memoir Series.

Text design by Eric Sawyer of Rose Design

I dedicate this book to

Mary, Pam, Jennifer,

Molly and Eva.

Whoever battles with monsters had better see that it does not turn him into a monster. And if you gaze long into an abyss, the abyss will gaze back into you.

—Friedrich Nietzsche

CONTENTS

LIST OF MAPS AND ILLUSTRATIONS

PREFACE

I slowly lowered the collective (pitch control) as we began our descent into Landing Zone Delta. All hell was breaking loose. The Firebird gunships were laying down cover as they screamed along side us. Their miniguns were puffing smoke, singing their loud, but familiar sound. Their rockets were yelling out loud, screaming sounds as they flew past. I told my crew, "Go hot." My crew chief and gunner unlocked their weapons and opened fire. The noise was deafening. Our helicopter felt as if it was coming alive from the shuddering and shaking from her guns. Tracers were flying in all directions. Fear and terror saturated the air.

We continued our descent down into the hell below. We already had two ships shot down and four more damaged by fire, but we continued. My crew chief yelled, "Taking fire at ten o'clock!" Then my gunner yelled, "Taking fire at one o'clock, no three o'clock. Hell, it's coming from everywhere!" We were now only three hundred yards from the landing zone and just about in, when I heard a loud explosion and felt the bird whine as a shell slammed through the transmission. The Huey reacted with a violent jolt, and then wham, another shell found its mark. I instantly pushed the cyclic forward and pulled up on the collective control, thinking to myself, "We're out of here." Fire was coming from everywhere and there was no place to hide. Time slowed to eternity as we slowly climbed out. Foot by foot, we distanced ourselves from the enemy and madness below.

We had taken a direct hit into the transmission, but thank God we were still flying. We could not set the bird down, it was too dangerous. We had to make it back, a little closer to the friendlies. Suddenly my crew chief yelled, "Mr. G, she's leaking bad, it doesn't look good." I took a quick look back over my right shoulder in the direction of the transmission. There was fluid running everywhere. It was time to make a decision.

~

Looking back on it, those moments of terror stand out in my mind for what it was like to be a combat helicopter pilot. *Rattler One-Seven* is a book about my tour in Vietnam. When I left for Vietnam, I was a nineteen-year-old Army helicopter pilot. I spent my entire Vietnam tour flying choppers. My tour started on May 15, 1970, and lasted through May 14, 1971. In the 1970s, I wrote down most of the high points of my adventures, when my memory was still clear with the facts and events.

I have written *Rattler One-Seven* as I experienced it, using my old letters written home to help keep the mindset I had when I was in Vietnam. I have included excerpts from some of the letters to reveal my feelings at the time about what I was experiencing. The grammar and spelling in the excerpts have been left as written. With age, you find out that your ideas and feelings about life change. I have tried very hard not to let my current feelings change the outlook that I had while actually experiencing these events.

Everyone who participated in the events that I talked about saw them in their own light. I have recounted the events as I saw and remember them. I am not alleging that the events took place in exactly the way that I explain them, only that this is the way that I remember them happening. I have changed some of the names for obvious reasons: government security, to protect them and their families and myself. Other names I have changed to protect the guilty.

At times, I have used derogatory terms to identify the North Vietnamese. Words such as Charlie, gook, and dink were common slang during the war, and I have kept them to keep the memoir historically accurate and to convey the feeling of the times. I intend no disrespect toward the Vietnamese people and apologize if it offends anyone.

I hope that reading *Rattler One-Seven* gives a realistic insight into what it was like to fly combat helicopters in Vietnam.

The author wishes to acknowledge and thank all the Rattlers and Firebirds with whom I spoke, especially Gary Arne, Pat Callahan, Don "Fat Rat" Lynam, and Kerry McMahon for their narratives. I also want to thank Doug Womack for his narrative and his vast knowledge of the history of our unit. Ron Seabolt, the National Director of the 71st Assault Helicopter Company Association, was a big help in locating members of the unit with whom I had lost contact after the war. I want to thank Wendell Freeman, Terry Wasson, and Larry Clampitt for sending me photos from their personal collection to be used in this book. Joe Kline, thank you for your beautiful cover art.

Working with Ron Chrisman at the University of North Texas Press has been a wonderful learning experience, and I thank him for all his time, questions, comments, and excellent editing that allowed this new author a chance to have his first book published.

I am grateful to Mary Gross, Paul Pecha, and Laura Sanders, for taking the time to review the manuscript and giving valuable input. I want to give a special thanks to my wife Pam and my daughters Jennifer and Molly for their loving support.

PROLOGUE—18 DAYS

Sitting here in the quiet solitude of my den, I find it hard to believe that the events that I am going to tell you about actually took place. When I reflect back upon them, they seem to be from another life, in another world, years ago. But they did happen, and I am thankful to be here today to tell about them.

Flying Captain for American Airlines on both the Boeing 767 and the 757 is a great job. It was my dream that I spent a better part of my life to achieve, yet I find it unfulfilling and boring compared to the flying experiences of my past. Yes, I have had a few emergencies at American in my career. I had an engine blow up on a Super 80 going into Minneapolis. Luckily, we set her down safely with no injuries. But losing an engine on an airliner is mild compared to the excitement of my past. Where should I begin?

It was late August of 1979. It had been a quick, short summer as summers are when you live in Minnesota. I was the Chief Pilot of an air cargo outfit called Crawford Aviation, Inc. Crawford Aviation's offices were located in Minneapolis, Minnesota, with our maintenance being performed at the Lake Elmo Airport. Our duties entailed flying freight for Airborne Airfreight.

Our fleet consisted of Beech 18 tail dragger aircrafts. The Beech 18 was first flown in 1937, and when World War Two started, the military placed large orders for the 18 in several different versions. They were used in an assortment of duties ranging from bombardier training to gunner training. They were also used as a light transport and for navigational training, and the navy used them in a photographic role. They were built after the war up to the mid-1960s.[1]

1. Chuck Gross standing in front of a Beech 18 at Janesville, Wisconsin. The Beech 18 was one of those aircraft in which you loved and hated to fly. (Author's collection.)

We had the later models called the Super 18. They had twin radial Pratt & Whitney R-985 AN-14B engines. These engines were air cooled and put out 450 horsepower each. The maximum gross weight was 9,700 pounds. They had a wingspan of 49 feet 8 inches and a length of 35 feet 2 1/2 inches.[2]

My main duty as Chief Pilot for Crawford Aviation was to hire and train our new pilots. We based our aircraft at the different cities that we served. The first leg of the night was to fly freight from that city into Chicago O'Hare Airport. At O'Hare, the pilot would park at the cargo ramp and unload his freight. He would then refuel and load up the outbound freight, which would be flown out to the different cities for overnight delivery.

I was in the process of checking out a new Beech 18 pilot by the name of Kevin Hoard. Kevin and I had grown up together, and I can never remember not knowing Kevin. We lived a block apart in a small neighborhood in Golden Valley, Minnesota. When I returned from Vietnam, Kevin was one of my first friends that I took up flying with me. He was so intrigued by that flight that, after a few years, he decided to get his ratings and pursue a career in aviation.

It was already past dark when Kevin and I arrived at the airplane. A check of the weather revealed a typical rainy, overcast night with rain showers scattered across the area. After completing our preflight checks, we taxied out and departed. We were flying along eastbound at an altitude of five thousand feet headed for O'Hare. I was in the right seat and Kevin was in the left. We were in the clouds flying by our instruments (which is called being in instrument meteorological conditions or IMC). We had been in the clouds since shortly after takeoff from Des Moines Airport and expected to stay in them till our descent into O'Hare. Kevin was still at the controls, piloting the plane. As I observed Kevin's flying, I happened to notice that with his one hand he was playing with a little map light that was attached to the control column. He was turning the adjustable lens back and forth when suddenly it sparked and the entire cockpit went dark.

I initially wasn't too worried. I knew that the overhead lights on the Beech 18 were always wired on a different circuit. With over fifteen hundred hours in the 18, I had grown accustomed to having mechanical problems, and had already had my fair share. I once had an electrical fire in the cockpit and had to declare an emergency, perform an emergency descent, and divert from my flight plan to land at the closest airport. I also had an engine jug blow on me one morning, forcing me to lose altitude and "baby" the aircraft to the airport. Luckily for me, the aircraft wasn't too heavily loaded or I would have had to set her down on a road or in a field. Life for a Beech 18 pilot was dangerous work.

I reached up to my overhead light and flicked the switch, but to my surprise the light did not come on! When flying under Federal Aviation Regulations part 135, you are required to carry a flashlight. I had noticed during the past few nights that my flashlight did not always come on when I tried to work it. I would just shake it, as we all have done, and it would work, so I really had not worried about it. But this time when I reached into my kit bag and tried out my flashlight, it came on and went right back out—no amount of shaking would make it work.

Thank goodness we were crossing over the city of Rockford, Illinois, and the reflection of the city lights off the clouds gave us enough light that I could barely make out the flight instruments. I instantly grabbed the controls from Kevin and started circling the aircraft to stay in the glow of the city lights. Our aircraft did not have an autopilot—without that glow we would be in total darkness, unable to maintain level flight and headed for a crash! As I grabbed the controls from Kevin, I yelled, "I got the controls, get your flashlight out." Kevin yelled back, "Sorry Chuck, I don't have one."

I knew that Kevin was a smoker, so I yelled at him to get his cigarette lighter out and light it. He dug into his pocket, pulled out his lighter, and clicked it. It initially lit, but due to the draftiness of the cockpit he could not keep it lit. As Kevin futilely attempted to keep his lighter lit, I checked the circuit breakers. I knew that all the electrical circuits were protected with breakers, so once I found the popped breaker, we could make sure that the map light was out, then push back in the popped breaker, and restore the lights. I ran my right hand across the circuit breaker panel, which was located right below the instrument panel, feeling for a popped circuit breaker, but to my dismay none were popped.

It was one of those nights where several small errors were working together in unison to create an accident. This is usually the case in most aviation accident investigations. There is normally not one major problem but a series of small problems that add up to becoming an accident. I could imagine the accident investigation team trying to figure out why an aircraft with plenty of fuel and both engines running suddenly spiraled out of control and crashed in a cornfield over Rockford, Illinois.

As I continued to circle the 18, I handed the flashlight to Kevin and told him to try to make it work. I then called center and declared an emergency. I told them what had happened, and told them that we would be circling in our present position.

While I was talking to center, Kevin had taken my flashlight apart and discovered that he could get it to light by holding the lens and bulb part of the flashlight to the batteries. With Kevin holding the flashlight together and pointing it towards my instrument panel, I called center and requested radar vectors for the Instrument Landing System (ILS) approach to the Rockford Airport. "Crawford 201, turn right heading 180, descend and maintain three thousand feet." "Crawford 201, turning right 180, we're out of five for three thousand." When we switched over to Rockford approach, they gave us a close turn into the final approach.

I wanted to get the aircraft on the ground as quickly as possible. I was not sure how long the flashlight would keep working. As I rolled out on final and intercepted the final approach course, I lowered the gear and configured the bird for landing. Crossing the final approach fix, I called the tower. "Rockford Tower, Crawford 201, marker in bound 36." "Roger Crawford 201, winds are 350 at six, cleared to land." As we descended through the clouds, flying by the light of a broken flashlight being held together by Kevin, I could feel that old familiar adrenalin rush that I had felt so many times during my tour of flying in Vietnam. It had been eight years since I had left Vietnam.

As we descended through the clouds, I decided that regardless of the ceiling and visibility, if we did not have the airport in sight, I would continue down below the landing minimums until we broke out or hit the runway. I figured it would be better to crash at the airport than in a field somewhere. But fortunately for us, the ceiling was lifting and we broke out and could see the airport. Kevin and I both breathed a sigh of relief. I landed the bird, and we taxied her to the ramp and shut her down. After further investigation, I discovered that there were two other main circuit breakers located under the copilot's seat and one of them was popped. Why they were located there, rather than with the other circuit breakers, I do not know. That was one of the problems with flying these older aircraft; every one of them was different. We made sure the map light was off, then we pushed the breaker back in and the entire cockpit's instrument lights came back on. I would have to talk with our maintenance and find out why they had wired the overhead lights to the same circuit as the flight instruments. Maybe they were that way when Crawford purchased the aircraft.

As I sat there in the cockpit, I thought to myself how ironic it would have been to have made it through my flying tour in Vietnam, surviving the special missions that I flew, surviving Lam Son 719, which was the most significant airmobile/air assault battle in Vietnam, only to end up crashing in a corn field outside Rockford, Illinois, because of maintenance personnel rewiring the cockpit lights wrong.

CHAPTER 1

FIRST ASSIGNMENT

It all started for me the summer of 1968. I had just graduated from Cooper High School in New Hope, Minnesota. I had decided against going to college. My mom suggested that I go into the service and get some training in electronics. Since I really had no clue as to what I wanted to do, the idea sounded good to me. My father had been an electrician before he passed away. The week after graduation, I went downtown to the U.S. Navy recruiter's office, where I took the usual battery of tests. When I had completed the tests, I was told to have a seat in the waiting room.

I was sitting in the waiting room with several other young men, while my tests were being graded, when a petty officer walked in and started yelling and screaming orders at us. He was cussing at us to stand up and get into formation. When I did not respond to his orders, he unleashed a mouthful of vulgarities at me. There was a little confusion as to who was who. The other men were new recruits who had just been given their oath, and he thought I was one of them. I have to admit, I was not used to all that vulgarity being directed at me, and it kind of shocked me. Once we got the confusion straightened out, he took his new recruits and lined them up. Yelling obscenities, he marched them out of the waiting room and down the corridor into their new life.

I was starting to have doubts about this navy idea when the recruiter called me into his office. He told me to take a seat. He then proceeded to tell me that I qualified for any navy school that I wanted, except electronics. He said my tests indicated that I had no aptitude for electronics. As I sat there listening to the recruiter, I quickly decided that I would kiss the idea about going into the navy goodbye. I told him thanks, but no thanks, and left. I was disappointed and not sure what I should do next. I had told all my friends, before graduation, that I was going in the navy and suddenly my plans were shot.

As I walked down the hallway towards the stairwell, I noticed a sign for the Army Recruiting Office. I decided to poke my head through the door. There was a sergeant sitting behind a desk and he said, "What can I do for you?"

I had a classmate in school whose father was an airline pilot. He had told us about his dad's job, and I thought that it sounded pretty cool. A friend of one of my brothers had a brother who had been flying helicopters in Vietnam for the army. Listening to Tom describe some of the letters that his brother had written home about his war experiences sounded exciting. So from out of nowhere, I told this sergeant, "I want to be an army pilot."

He told me to come in. He had me take a battery of tests similar to the tests I had just taken at the Navy Recruiting Office. After the sergeant reviewed my results, he told me I qualified to take the warrant officer (WO) written flight test. There was one problem. I was too young. I had to be eighteen to take the test and I was only seventeen. I set up an appointment to take the test on August 15, which was my eighteenth birthday. Within just a few hours, my life had taken a new direction.

Early on the morning of August 15, I got up and drove down to take the written flight test. I was anxious because I had only been in an airplane once as a twelve year old for a short ten-minute ride. I had no knowledge of how an airplane flew or how to interpret what the flight instruments were telling me in the test that I took. Seven of us took the test that morning. After completing the test, we were sent to a waiting room to wait for our grades.

Once the grading was completed, the recruiter started calling names one at a time. When a name was called, that individual would get up and go into the sergeant's office, and they would close the door. Then the rest of us would wait until he left and the next name was called. When the recruiter called the sixth name, I was the only one left in the waiting room. I began to worry. It had been a tough test and, with my lack of aviation knowledge, I knew that I had guessed at several of the answers.

After what seemed like hours, my name was called. I got up and walked into the sergeant's office. He told me to have a seat. As he reviewed my tests, he shook his head from side to side. He then told me that I didn't pass the test. He explained that I needed a score of 250 to pass and I had only gotten 248. He then asked me, "How bad do you want this?" I emphasized, "I've really been counting on doing this!" He looked at me and then looked down at my results, tapping his pencil on the desk. Then after a long silent moment, he said, "Hell, they're going to teach you everything you need to know in flight school anyways." I watched as he took his pencil and erased the 248 and wrote down 251. I thought to myself, "What a birthday present!" I told him thanks, and then we scheduled an appointment for the board. We were required to interview in front of a board of officers before being accepted into the Warrant Officer Rotary Wing Aviation Course (WORWAC). Warrant officer was a rank below the commissioned officers but above the enlisted grades. There were four grades of warrant officer starting with WO1 through WO4, with WO4 being the highest. Warrant officers were entitled to a salute from the enlisted personnel and called "mister."

I can still hear the officer in charge of the interview for WORWAC. At the conclusion of the interview he stated, "You realize that upon completion of the course, you will receive orders to Vietnam." I stated, "Yes, I do." What was the Vietnam conflict to me? I was only eighteen years old and had never been out of the States. I had seen news clippings of the war on TV so it was nothing new to me. The news was always showing footage of the fighting and killing. With the rebellions, protests, riots, violence and crime in the early and mid-1960s, it had become a way of life. Besides, I thought the war would be over by the time I had completed my training.

My military career started on November 25, 1968. I was eager for the adventure and excitement of combat that I had seen so many times at the movies and on television, with all the heroics and glories of victory. But I was soon to find out the other qualities of war that the movies and tube had failed to show. I completed flight school on

November 4, 1969, at Hunter Army Airfield in Savannah, Georgia. I received my wings and graduated as a warrant officer in the United States Army. I had an all too short tour of duty at Fort Carson, Colorado, and then received my orders to Vietnam. My departure was scheduled for May 15, 1970. I would be leaving the country from McCord Air Force Base near Seattle, Washington.

The sun was breaking over the horizon when my wake-up call came. It was the fifteenth. I had flown into Seattle the night before. I checked into the Hilton and went to bed early so that I would be fresh for the day. This was one day that I did not want to be late. I grabbed a cab for the airport where I could catch a bus that ran to McCord. It was during this bus ride that I started feeling excited about the future and what it had in store for me. But along with this feeling of excitement, there was another feeling that radiated from deep down inside of my bones. It felt like a heavy weight anchored in my lower stomach. I had this same type of feeling in my high school speech class, when I would stand up in front of the class and speak.

Upon arriving at McCord Air Force Base, I immediately checked into the transportation terminal. The time was approaching 1000 hours, but there were few people in sight. I found a bench to rest on and began what was a long and boring wait.

As I sat there thinking, the same thought kept running through my mind. "If only it was a year from now!" The standard length of tour for Vietnam was one year. One year is a very long period of time when you are only nineteen. I thought to myself, "A year from now, it will be the happiest day of my life!"

Around noon, I rode over to the Officer's Club and got a bite to eat. When I got back from lunch, more soldiers were starting to fill the terminal. As I scanned the room, I could tell that they were not a happy bunch. It was not long before one of the other warrant officer pilots and I had started a conversation. He introduced himself as Buddy Howard. He was born and raised in Tennessee, as his heavy accent indicated. Being from the midwest, there was quite a difference in the way we spoke. In the army, when we would meet a fellow aviator, the conversation would always get around to which flight class we graduated from. I found out Buddy had been in the same class as my good friend Dave Warman, with whom I had been stationed in

Colorado. Our mutual friendship with Dave sparked an almost instant comradeship as we talked and got to know each other. Dave and Buddy had been quite close in flight school. Dave had received his orders to Nam a couple of weeks after I had, so I was not able to contact him again after leaving Colorado. A few hours later Bob, a good friend of Buddy's, arrived, and the three of us hit it right off. This new friendship was going to help immensely during the next few days.

Throughout the afternoon and into the evening, we watched other soldiers depart and return, but our flight did not take off until later that night. It was around 2200 hours that night that they finally lined us up to board the aircraft. The aircraft was a Seaboard World 707. This was the aircraft that was going to take us to a world so different from the one we knew. It was a long, tiring flight, which lasted over eighteen hours. The Boeing 707 made only two fuel stops in Anchorage, Alaska, and then in Okinawa. Since I had gotten up early that morning, I was tired and tried to sleep on the plane. The little rest I did manage to get on the plane was not very refreshing.

I could feel my body's temperature rise and my heartbeat quicken when the captain's voice came over the intercom announcing the beginning of our descent into Cam Ranh Bay. Not really knowing what to expect, everyone on the aircraft was stretching and leaning to get their first look at what was going to be our new home. Our landing at Cam Ranh Bay was uneventful. Cam Ranh Bay was a secured Air Force Base. The most excitement they ever experienced was an occasional rocket or sapper attack. Cam Ranh Bay was the main entry and departure point for U.S. forces. Here the soldiers were processed into the country and sent to their unit of assignment.

It had been Friday when my day had started, and I think it was Sunday when we finally arrived. I would find out after arriving at my unit that all the days were going to be the same. I would never really be sure what day of the week it would be, but I would always know the date. There would always be someone counting down the days to his date of estimated return from overseas (DEROS). The only special days during my tour were going to be Christmas, New Years, and my DEROS date. The DEROS date was the most important. It was the date that you lived for the whole year, the day that you would get to go home.

We were met at the plane by an army bus. As I walked down the steps from the aircraft to the tarmac, the heat was the first thing that got my attention. It had been the first blossoming of spring when I had left Minnesota and now, suddenly, this hot humid air was engulfing my lungs. It would take quite a few days for my body to adjust to the heat and humidity. Then there was that awful smell! It was something that I had never smelled before. The smell was a combination of urine, gunpowder, oriental food, and garbage. Upon entering the army bus, we noticed bars on the windows. The bars were not to keep us from getting out, but to stop someone from throwing grenades or explosives into the bus.

Our bus took us from the airfield over to the processing center. We would end up spending a day and a half at the processing center waiting for our assignments. This day and a half wait was a very hard and emotional time for us. We were all eager to get to our units. The inactivity and the sitting around with nothing to do to pass the time made it worse. Bob, Buddy, and I stayed together during this time, trying to catch up on our sleep. It had been a long couple of days and we were tired. When I woke up, I went over to the showers to wash. I was standing in the shower when a couple of Vietnamese women walked in and started washing clothes. I thought this was kind of strange to have grown women washing clothes while I stood there stark naked, but they did not seem to mind, so neither did I.

For some unexplained reason, it was always the middle of the night when we did our traveling. It was 0200 hours, and we were standing in line to load onto a C-130 transport. Our new destination was Chu Lai. Chu Lai was located in I Corps and was the home of the Americal Division, an area that was becoming well known back in the States due to the My Lai Massacre. (The Americal Division was formed in 1942 during World War II in New Caledonia. It is said that the people of Caledonia liked the Americans so much that the name was formed by a contraction of AMERIcans and CALedonia. When the division was reactivated during Vietnam it was designated the 23rd Infantry Division.) Chu Lai would become my home for the next eight months. It was early morning by the time we landed at Chu Lai and exited the C-130. Chu Lai looked quite different from Cam Ranh Bay. Looking off to the west, I could see a barren, brownish, massive ridge running north and south along the skirts of the base. Over to the east, paralleling the ridge was the coast of the South China Sea. That first sighting of the barren ridge would stay in my mind for years to come. Why? I would never really know. After unloading the aircraft, we were taken by jeep to another reception center set up by the Americal Division. This was an indoctrination school in which all new arrivals into this division were required to attend. We were to spend the next five days learning about the different aspects of Vietnam.

These few days were some of the best days of my tour. At this point, we were not really active in the war and we were eager to move on, not knowing what lay in store for us. We were taken to our quarters. Built with stick lumber, they had plywood floors with tin roofs, and screens running from the roof halfway down the sides to join the plywood knee wall. Inside these so-called barracks were double bunks lined up on both sides of the building. Everyone in Vietnam called this type of building a hootch. The area around this reception center was very sandy and hilly due to it being situated right off the South China Beach. Bob, Buddy, and I were assigned the same hootch. We had a briefing scheduled for the officers later in the afternoon. Since we had been up all night, we spent the rest of the morning catching up on our sleep.

In my first official Vietnam briefing, I was introduced to the different areas in which the Americal Division operated. Even as I sat there listening to the briefing, it was still hard for me to realize that I was actually in Vietnam. During my first night in Chu Lai, I received my initial taste of the war. After our briefing, we ate dinner and had the rest of the evening to ourselves. The reception center had a movie screen set up outside with several wooden benches. This makeshift theater was located back in the southwestern corner of the reception center and would show movies every night. Because there was very little to do, we ended up watching *The Sterile Cuckoo.* They started the show right after sunset, and it ran until about 2130 hours. After the movie, we headed for the sack.

I had just fallen asleep when I heard a commotion coming from underneath my bunk. I heard a noise that sounded like someone was rummaging through my stuff. I stretched my neck out from my bunk and looked down at my belongings. I had left a bag of M&Ms sitting in my bag and, to my surprise, there was a huge lizard dragging off my candy. He was about twenty-four inches long and ugly. I quickly decided that he could have the candy. I carefully tucked my legs and arms back under my blanket, rolled over, and went back to sleep.

I had been off in dreamland quite some time when a loud, screaming whistle broke the silence. Immediately following the scream was a loud explosion, followed by another. As the second explosion still echoed in my ears, I shot up and jetted out of the hootch, making tracks for the nearest bunker. Buddy was running right alongside me. The two of us had almost made it to the bunker when we saw, to our amazement, Bob running in the wrong direction. Buddy and I quickly reversed direction and ran after him. Screaming and yelling, we chased after Bob until we caught his attention. Then the three of us changed direction and made tracks back to the bunker. I came to find out that Bob was still half asleep when we had caught up with him. He had known enough to run, just not where. We all thought it was funny and had a good laugh about it. We stayed in the bunker until the rockets stopped and then headed back to the hootch. This had been our first real indication of the war. I think that more soldiers were injured running for cover from the rockets than from the actual explosions.

The next morning in our briefing we were told that Chu Lai had been receiving a few rockets and mortars every night for the past week. I discovered that this was quite a common occurrence. The next few days we attended classes during the day and watched movies in the evening. The classes were mainly on Vietnamese customs, warfare, and tactics.

One of the most interesting and amazing topics in the classes was a demonstration given by a Kit Carson Scout. A Kit Carson Scout was an ex-Viet Cong who had rallied to the South Vietnamese government and begun to soldier for them. This class was scheduled after dark to demonstrate the effectiveness of a sapper. A sapper was a soldier whose mission was to sneak in through the perimeter of an enemy's compound and blow up preselected targets. They had an area with a simulated perimeter set up specifically for this class. Approximately twenty yards long and fifteen yards wide, it was covered with barbed wire strung across the surface, with coils of concertina wire stretched out on top of the barbed wire. Attached to the wire were tin cans hanging down to alert us to the slightest movement. They began the class by having the sapper strip down to a pair of dark shorts. He then wrapped a sack filled with satchel charges around his waist. This, we were told, was the extent of a sapper's uniform. As we looked on, we all felt quite secure that no one could make it through that mess of wires without making a noise that would alert us. Our false confidence in this wired perimeter was soon shattered. The scout began his penetration of the perimeter crawling on his belly. With one hand, and then the other, he would pick and lift the wire snaking his body back and forth, quickly working his way through that hell of a tangled mess. In and out, down and through the wire he maneuvered. It took him less than sixty seconds to crawl through the perimeter without making the slightest sound, destroying any security we felt this type of perimeter offered. It definitely got the point across.

The following morning our unit assignments came down. Buddy and Bob were assigned to the 174th Aviation Company, located south of Chu Lai. I was assigned to the Americal Division, 14th Combat Aviation Battalion (CAB), 71st Assault Helicopter Company (AHC), stationed right at Chu Lai. Finally, we were going to get into action. I felt sad that I was not going with Buddy and Bob. Emotionally, it would have been easier to go to a new unit with them, but I was accustomed to parting with friends by now. That always happened in the service. As soon as you really got to know and like someone, you were saying goodbye. After parting with Buddy and Bob, I threw my equipment into the jeep and hopped in. The driver shifted into first gear and off we headed to the 71st AHC.

CHAPTER 2

COMPANY CHECKOUT

We headed out on Sunday, May 24, 1970, for the home base of the 71st Assault Helicopter Company. It was a dry, sandy road, and our jeep left a light cloud of dust as we traveled down it. The company area was situated along the South China Beach, about a mile from the Chu Lai airstrip. As we traveled down the dirt road, my mind ran wild with excitement. Changing units was a lot like moving to a new job. You are excited about the future and what it has in store for you, yet you are also sad and lonely, for it is not easy to re-adjust and make new friends. As our jeep pulled around the bend, I saw the South China Sea. It had the most beautiful, glistening, white sandy beach that I had ever seen. I instantly felt the cooling breeze coming off the water as it swept across my face.

Our driver pulled into the company area and stopped in front of the orderly room. I jumped out and pulled my gear out of the jeep. One of the first things you were required to do upon arriving at your new unit was to report to the orderly room and sign in. Being as trustworthy as I was, I set my equipment down outside and entered the orderly room. I pulled my orders out and presented them to the company clerk. He looked them over and told me to sign in. I reported to the commanding officer, Major Tommie James. Major James welcomed me to the unit and gave me a short briefing of the 71st operations.

The 71st was part of the 14th CAB and would fly support for both the 196th Light Infantry Brigade and the 2nd Army Republic of Vietnam (ARVN) Division. The tactics used in Vietnam were different from the tactics used in previous wars. Rather than trying to acquire territory, our goal in Vietnam was to locate and destroy the enemy and their supplies. Once the enemy was found, our troops relied on artillery and air strikes to help destroy them. These missions were called search-and-destroy missions. Due to this type of tactic, our area of operation (AO) had several fire-support bases (FSB) to give the necessary artillery support. Another concept that was introduced in Vietnam warfare was air mobility. The army would use the helicopter to transport the troops and their supplies while working in their AO. When the enemy was located, helicopters quickly transported the infantry soldiers into battle. These insertions were referred to as combat assaults. Air mobility was the job of the 71st AHC.

When Major James finished my briefing, I was shown to my new quarters, where I was assigned a corner section of a hootch similar to the ones that we had been staying in previously, only these hootchs were a little smaller and they had partitions set up between the bunks. A bunk and a small locker were the extent of my furniture.

When I returned to the orderly room to pick up my belongings, I noticed that my flight helmet was gone. Someone had stolen it. At this point, I began to realize this was going to be a different world from what I was accustomed. I immediately reported the theft to the orderly room. Even though I was new to the company and had yet to meet anyone, I felt a strong reaction to the theft of my helmet. It was hard not to take a theft personally. It did not take the first sergeant long to find out who had stolen my helmet. He appeared to be well acquainted with what was happening in the company area. A couple of enlisted men had done the dirty deed. The first sergeant felt that because the helmet was returned, no harm was done, and no punishment was needed. This did not sit right with me, but since I was new to the unit I felt it was best not to make a fuss. This incident did not make me feel very welcome to my new home.

After my helmet was returned, I was taken for a tour of the company area, and was shown the location of the supply office where I would be getting the rest of my equipment. I saw where the mess hall, the outhouses, and the showers were located. I briefly met the pilots who were not flying and then received the rest of the day off to unpack and get my belongings in order. Tomorrow I would go to the division supply where I would receive another pair of combat boots, a newer model flight helmet, two Nomex flight suits, and two sets of Nomex flight gloves. Nomex was a nonflammable fabric that would afford at least some protection against an aircraft fire.

Another new warrant officer (WO) pilot arrived later that afternoon. He was assigned to the same hootch as me but at the opposite end. Since we were both new to the 71st, we introduced ourselves and started to talk. He introduced himself as Kent Garrett. As we sat there talking, I did not realize at that time that Garrett was going to strongly influence my attitude toward the Vietnam War. Garrett hailed from Colorado and was my elder by seven years. He told me that he was married and had a young son. My first impression of Kent was that he was nice and friendly, yet reserved.

While Garrett and I sat in our hootch getting to know each other, one of the other WO pilots came in to talk. His name was James McCarragher. I could tell by his accent that he was Canadian. He wanted to make sure that we understood some of the company's policies concerning newbies. Newbie was the nickname they used to call the new guys in the company. McCarragher went on to explain since we were newbies we would be required to do anything the senior pilots wanted us to do. For instance, if one of the pilots woke up in the middle of the night and was thirsty, we were required to get up, run down to the mess hall, and get him a glass of water. I told him, "You can just wait and see." I did not care how new I was; I was not going to be someone's gopher. I knew better than to start that crap.

I spent the rest of the day and early evening meeting the other pilots as they came back from flying. I finished unpacking the few belongings I had. I had just completed getting everything unpacked, when one of the enlisted men came into my hootch. He walked directly up to me and pulled out his knife and stuck it a few inches from my face. He acted as if he might use it on me. Looking in his eyes, I could tell that he was high on something. As he stood there waving his knife in front of my face, my stomach started to tense and turn sour. I knew better than to show it. I said to him, "Give me the knife, and I'll show you how to use it." At that point, he quit waving the knife and stared at me for a moment. He said, "Mr. Gross, you're all right." Then he turned and stumbled away. I thought to myself, "They sure have a funny way of welcoming a new guy to this unit!" I figured I had earned his respect and left it at that.

The next morning, I ran into one of the pilots in our unit that I had been stationed with during basic training. His name was Steve Israel. While I had been fortunate enough to get stateside duty upon completion of flight school, Israel had received orders directly to Nam. He had already been there for about six months. Israel also happened to be one of the unit's instructor pilots. In Nam we called everyone by his last name. It was a military custom.

It was very refreshing to see a familiar face. It had been over a year since we had last talked, so we stood there and shot the breeze for a few minutes. Israel scheduled my company aircraft checkout with him for early afternoon. I immediately headed up to the division supply office to get my flight equipment, grabbed some lunch, and then headed back down to the flight line for my flight check. I thought my checkout was going to be a little easier because I already knew the instructor pilot. Boy, was I mistaken.

The 71st AHC aircraft were UH1-D/H Iroquois, manufactured by Bell Helicopter. The nickname of the UH1 (utility helicopter) was "Huey," coming from the pronunciation of the original U.S. Army UH-1 designation. The Huey became synonymous with the Vietnam War and would become the greatest military helicopter of all time. The D/H models we were flying in 1970 were phase two of the Huey. They stretched the fuselage by approximately three feet. This larger volume added about 12 percent more capacity to the Huey from the earlier B/C models. Those early B models had a 960hp T53 engine, whereas the C models had an 1100hp T53-L-11 turbine engine. In the H model, they increased the power of the turbine to 1400-hp using an Avco Lycoming T53-L-13 turboshaft engine. The H model had an empty weight of 5,200 lbs and a maximum take-off weight of 9,480 lbs. It would carry about 3,870 lbs of freight. It had a maximum speed of 127 mph with a range of 315 miles at sea level. Its fuselage was 41 feet 10 inches in length, with a height of 14 feet 6 inches. The main rotor diameter was 48 feet. The U.S. Army purchased from Bell a total of 9,440 Hueys of all models—5,435 of which were UH-1Hs.[3]

Israel started my checkout with a preflight, which consisted of a walk-around inspection of the aircraft. He asked me about nearly every item on the aircraft. Then we went up for my flight check. My flying was not too bad, but my knowledge of the instrument limitations was weak, and Israel made a point of emphasizing that weakness. He went over each engine instrument, asking me the maximum and minimum limitations allowed. It was embarrassing to tell Israel that I didn't know the answer to some of the questions that he was asking, especially since he was a friend. I passed the checkout, but my pride was hurt. I promised myself that from now on, I would commit to memory all the limitations of the Huey and never forget them. Never again

2. Warrant Officer Steve Israel. Steve and I had taken our basic training together at Fort Polk, Louisiana. (Photo courtesy of Don Lynam.)

would I allow myself to be embarrassed like this in front of an instructor pilot (IP). I realized he did this for my own good and I would learn from the experience.

My third day with the 71st was the day I had been waiting for, the day I would finally get to fly combat. The flight assignments were always completed the night before for the pilots. Operations would pair the pilots with the copilots and assign the gunner. The crew chief and aircraft were not assigned until early morning. This allowed maintenance to work on the birds during the night and allowed operations more time to decide which aircraft would be available for flight. For my first day of flying, I was assigned to fly with Israel. When I found out, I felt relieved. I knew on the first day there would be so much to learn, and I would not have to worry about getting to know a different pilot.

I woke up at 0430 hours and got dressed. I went over to the mess hall, ate a quick breakfast, and caught the truck by 0510 hours. The truck would take us down to our flight line. It was about a twelve-minute ride from our company area to the flight line. When we arrived at the flight line, Israel dropped into operations and checked the board to see which aircraft we would be flying. We went out to the helicopter, or "bird," as we called it in the service.

We immediately started our preflight, checking over the entire bird to make sure that every moveable part was within limitations and looked safe for flight. We also checked to make sure that the fluid levels in the main transmission and tail rotor gearbox were full. When we arrived at our bird, our gunner was already at work checking out his guns and making sure that they were in working order with the proper amount of ammunition. Once we completed the preflight, we cranked up the bird and departed for our first assignment. The flight crews always tried to lift off from the flight line by 0600 hours.

In Vietnam the aircraft commander, who we called the AC, flew from the left seat. The copilot flew from the right. Most helicopters like the Huey were designed to fly from the right seat, but in the actual experience of combat flying in Vietnam, the army discovered that it was advantageous for the AC to fly the Huey from the left seat. Visibility was very important when flying in Vietnam, especially when flying low-level or trying to land in a tight landing zone. Because of the way the instrument panel was designed in the Huey, you had better visibility in the left seat versus the right. Our standard approach into a LZ was a high overhead approach, which was a steep descending turn. Due to the aerodynamics of the helicopter, it was better to execute a high overhead approach in a left turn instead of right. Being the AC, you wanted to be on the side of the aircraft in which you were making the turn, which allowed you to see better what was taking place on the ground as you shot your approach.

Our crew consisted of four members: two pilots, a crew chief, and a gunner. The crew chief's duties were to help maintain the bird and operate—while flying—one of the two .30-cal. M60 machine guns mounted on each side of the aircraft at the back of the main cabin doors. The gunner was responsible for maintaining the M60s and operating the other gun during flight. The copilot and gunner would change daily, but once you made AC you were assigned a bird with a crew chief, and you would try to stay with your bird as much as you could. Thus you would get to know the aircraft and become good friends with your crew chief.

On my first day of combat flying, we flew resupply for an infantry unit in our brigade. We began by loading up our bird with supplies at Hawk Hill, where the brigade's headquarters was located. We took the supplies and flew them out to the company's main unit, located in our area of operations at a fire-support base. A fire-support base was a small base strategically located on the top of a hill or high ground for good defense. The typical fire-support base had several bunkers built into the hill, with a strong perimeter set up to keep the sappers out. They would have several artillery pieces set up to give artillery support to the infantry troops in their AO. The fire-support bases always had a helicopter pad to send and receive supplies by air.

From the fire-support base, we flew supplies to individual platoons located out in the field. The supplies consisted of C-rations, ammunitions, and anything else that the ground units needed while operating out in the field. I realized very quickly that I was going to have to forget everything I had learned stateside about flying tactical combat. Here in Vietnam I would have to learn all new techniques.

Israel spent a good part of the morning giving me an excellent orientation of our AO. I got to fly a little straight and level and try a couple of approaches. My first two approaches were disastrous. I had

3. A C-Model Firebird gunship with rocket pods and miniguns being prepared for battle. (Photo courtesy of Wendell Freeman.)

never had a chance to fly a helicopter that was fully loaded in such strong, gusty winds. My lack of experience showed. When we flew the birds in flight school, they were empty. Israel told me, "Don't let it bother you, Chuck. It's natural to have problems the first few days." It did bother me, for I always took great pride in my flying and now I felt like I was starting over. Confidence is one of the major factors in flying helicopters, and mine was disappearing quickly.

When I first arrived in Vietnam, my dream was to fly gunships. There were two types of helicopters used as gunships in Vietnam: the C model Hueys, which were set up with rockets, miniguns, and sometimes grenade launchers; and the Bell AH-1 Cobra. The Cobra was the first helicopter designed from its infancy as a rotorcraft gunship. It had tandem seating, in which the pilot sat in back and the gunner sat down in front so that they both had a clear view of the battlefield. It had stubby little wings on its side that were used to carry many of its weapons. The Cobra had four hard points in which rocket pods and missiles were attached to the wings, and it carried a six-barrel minigun in its nose. This minigun could fire up to 100 rounds per second.[4] Both the Huey and the Cobra reaped massive destruction upon the enemy. In our unit, we had the C model gunships.

When I first arrived at the 71st, I immediately put in my request to fly gunships. I was told that I would have to first start out as a "Slick Pilot." After a period of flying slicks, I would be able to transfer over to the guns. A "slick" was a term used to describe the flying done by the UH-1 D/H model Huey. The slick's mission consisted of flying resupply (referred to as "ash and trash"), combat assaults, aerial observation, psychological operations, spraying Agent Orange, and special operations. The gun pilots and the slick pilots acted as if they were two different classes of people, and there appeared to be a big divide between the two groups. The 71st had two lift platoons and one gun platoon. Since the gun pilots had their own platoon they had their own hootchs. They did not really socialize with the slicks that much. Competition seemed to exist between the two groups.

During my first day of flying, I told Israel that I wanted to fly guns. He told me he did not think that I would feel the same way after I took a few weeks to get to know and understand the operations of both types of flying. In his opinion, slicks were better pilots than guns because they flew a lot more and shot a lot more approaches. Whereas the gun pilots were always stuck flying circles waiting to lay down their firepower, the slicks were constantly flying in and out of the landing zones (LZ). Furthermore, it took a certain type of mentality to be a gun pilot.

I found the first couple of weeks of flying very frustrating and difficult. I was trying to make emotional adjustments far greater than anything that I had ever experienced before. The flying itself was hard enough, but then you add in the long days, the little sleep, the different diet, the hot weather, and then throw in trying to fit in with the other guys. It was tough. I found out that next to flying, fitting in with the guys as a newbie would be the hardest adjustment to make. As a newbie, you received little respect and lots of harassment.

CHAPTER 3

NEWBIE

My watch indicated 0500 hours as I climbed into the back of our company truck for the shuttle down to our flight line. I had barely gotten into the truck when I started hearing everyone shouting, "Newbie, newbie." They also had other nicknames for us, such as "Peter Pilot" and "Meat in the Seat." By the time I finished flying the first day, I would understand why they came up with the term "Meat in the Seat."

During your first few weeks of flying, when you were new in country, your learning curve was very steep. There was a lot of action taking place in the cockpit, but as a new guy, you were sitting there in the copilot seat basically doing nothing but occupying space. You did not have a clue as to what was happening. From this emotional state of numbness came the term "Meat in the Seat," because that was about all you were good for your first week. During my first day of flying out in the AO, I had a hard time just understanding the radios. My aircraft commander (AC) was listening to two, sometimes three radios at the same time. He had no problem understanding it at all. He had developed the knack of knowing what to expect and when to expect it from each channel. To me, it sounded like one loud garbled blur. As I sat there listening to this commotion, I was truly amazed that my AC had no problem talking on both radios simultaneously, switching back and forth between the radios as he spoke.

In the 71st Assault Helicopter Company there appeared to be three groups of pilots, or should I say cliques. The ACs who flew the slicks formed the first group under the call sign of the Rattlers, the gunship pilots the second under the call sign of the Firebirds, and the copilots made up the third and lowly group. I quickly noticed that the three groups did not intermingle socially. I was really amazed and dumbfounded at how you would spend all day flying with an aircraft commander and as soon as the flying day was complete, that same AC would head back to his clique and he would have nothing to do with you.

Back in our company area, the big thing to do when you were not flying was to drink, and believe me, excessive amounts of drinking occurred nightly. When I first arrived at our company, I noticed that every night after the ACs got tanked up they would go hunting for newbies to harass. One of their favorite tricks was what they called the aerial drop—bombing the newbie with sandbags. They would look for a sleeping newbie, sneak into his hootch, and do an aerial drop on him. After watching this happen a few times to the other new pilots, I began to wonder when I would become the target of their nightly bombings. I started to sleep with one eye open. I was lucky that I personally was never harassed that much. Some of the other new guys who came into our company around my time were less fortunate. I lost many an hour of sleep listening to the yelling and screaming of those drunken pilots as they went around on their nightly missions of newbie harassment.

I had been in our company about two weeks when we had two new pilots assigned to our unit. Both of them were very young, nineteen or maybe twenty years old. Instantly, the slick ACs began harassing these poor guys. They were both assigned to the hootch next to us, and initially I did not pay that much attention to them. The following night I was walking over to take a shower, when suddenly one of the new pilots came flying out one of the windows of their hootch, as if he were superman. The other new guy was close on his tail. They were both drunker than a sailor on shore leave. They jumped up and ran towards the beach, yelling and screaming as they went. Right behind them came five or six of our ACs in hot pursuit. The ACs had these poor guys running all day and into the night. I did not know when they got any sleep. I quickly learned as a newbie, you had to let them know from the start that you would not be playing their games and doing all the chores they wanted you to do. These poor guys had not figured that out yet.

A few nights later, around 0030 hours, the slick ACs decided that since they had such a large group of new pilots, about eight of us, it was time to have a newbie party to initiate us. All of these drunken

ACs put their heads together and came up with the idea to make the newbies a special drink for the occasion. Their plan was to get us drunk and make us as sick as possible. They began by mixing up a concoction of beer and hard liquor, then salad dressing, and finally anything else that they could find drinkable. Once they had this special drink mixed, they started inviting newbies over for drinks.

Luckily for me, this special event was taking place in the next hootch over rather than in our hootch. I could tell from all the yelling and screaming that they would be coming for us shortly. They began their party by rounding up all the newbies that lived in their hootch, telling them that they had no choice but to join the party, and then forcing them to drink this special concoction. After they got the first group of newbies drunk, it was time to recruit more newbies, so they headed over to our hootch. I had a new guy that lived right across the hall from me, named Paul Grubbs. Grubbs had already been drinking earlier, so they easily carried him off in the direction of the party. Next, they came for Kent Garrett. Garrett said he would not go. They told him, "Either come of your own free will or we'll physically carry you over." Garrett, being no fool, got up and went with them.

So there I was, lying in my bunk, waiting for my personal invitation to go to this great party. As I lay there listening to all the commotion from next door, I looked at my watch. It was already after 0130 hours. I decided that I was too tired for this crap. I did not go in for this kind of harassment, since I didn't drink that much, and besides, I was scheduled to fly in about four hours. So I picked up a ball-peen hammer that I had noticed earlier under my bunk and tucked it inside my sleeping bag. I decided that I would nail the first person that came through my door. I figured they were all so drunk that they would never know what hit them. It may sound quite harsh now, but at the time when you are tired and trying to get to sleep it seemed perfectly logical. Then I tried to get some sleep. Luckily, by the time they got Garrett over to the party, everyone was so drunk that they forgot about me. The next morning, on our ride down to the flight line, Israel mentioned that he did not remember seeing me at the party last night. I just sat there silently. I knew by the time it came around for the next newbie party, I would no longer be a newbie and just one of the regular guys. In the 71st, everyone believed that these parties, along with the newbie harassment, were great for morale. This may had been the case for the old guys, but not for the new guys.

During my first few months in the 71st AHC, it was our company's tradition to hold award ceremonies. In these ceremonies, the company commander would get up in front of the pilots and present plaques to the pilots who were finishing their tours. These plaques were carved in the shape of aviator wings, with a brass plate attached showing the pilot's name and the number of hours flown in combat. I thought that they were neat and I really looked forward to getting mine. Unfortunately for me, by the time that I got to this point in my tour, our commanding officer (CO) had done away with the wings.

At these awards ceremonies, there was always a lot of drinking in celebration of the old guys completing their tour. After finishing the ceremonies, the pilots would always grab a new AC or copilot and "aircraft carrier" qualify him. It was at this point in the evening that Garrett and I would start heading for the door. We knew what was coming, so we always had our escape route planned. We did not feel the need to become carrier qualified.

The pilot who was picked to be carrier qualified would usually try to make his getaway. Being outnumbered, he would be captured and by sheer physical force carried back to the staging field. First, the pilots would build a "carrier deck" of cardboard pieces ten feet long on the concrete floor. If cardboard was not available, they would do it right on the concrete. At the far end of the makeshift carrier deck, they would stack a pile of beer cans as high as they could. The second step was to wet down the cardboard or cement flight deck with beer. The third and final step in preparation for this big event was to get a bunch of guys to urinate into a spray fire extinguisher and mix it with beer. Then, while a group of guys held the chosen pilot aloft, they would spray him down with this mixture of urine and beer. On the count of three, the pilots would throw him down this so-called carrier deck into the beer cans. At that point, he was considered carrier qualified.

If you did not go in for this type of fun, it was a lot harder to fit in with the boys. I had a very high opinion of man when I came to Vietnam, but as my tour passed, I was to form an entirely different opinion. I am sorry to say that it was not a very good one.

We got awfully tired of being called newbie all the time. Besides playing tricks on the newbies in the company area, the crews also liked to play tricks on them while they were flying. When I first arrived at the 71st AHC, the gunners were allowed to disconnect their M60s from the aircraft's fixed gun mounts. They then mounted their guns to big bungee cords, which removed the limited degree of movement built into the gun mount and allowed the gunners more versatility when firing. (Later in my tour, the practice of using the bungee cords would be outlawed because too many gunners got carried away while shooting. They got target fixation and were so focused on shooting the enemy that they would accidentally shoot their own bird, usually hitting it in the rotor blades.)

But for now, it was standard practice to have the M60s hanging from the bungee cords. One of the tricks that the crew liked to play on a new copilot was when the AC told them to go hot (a term the AC used to tell his crew to start firing their weapons), the gunner on the right side of the aircraft would work his way up with the gun towards the front of the aircraft, right behind the copilot's seat. The gunner would then angle his gun so that the hot empty casings being discharged would eject and hit the back of the copilot's neck. This definitely got the copilot's attention, and everyone thought it was funny. Welcome to Vietnam!

When you were new in country, during your initial briefing, one of the first things they warn you to do is to make sure you take your malaria pills, to protect you from getting malaria. The only problem was that the pill tended to give you diarrhea when you first started taking them. Luckily for me, I had a few guys warn me about their effect, so I decided not to bother taking the pills. There could be no worst feeling than to have the runs while flying helicopters in Nam. You could not just pull into a Seven Eleven and run in to use the john.

We got this new warrant officer assigned to our company, named Robert Terry (name changed). I guess no one bothered to tell Robert about the effects of taking the malaria pills, or else he chose to ignore the warning. Being a good soldier, Terry took his malaria pills and went flying. What a big mistake! Sure enough, he got diarrhea. There was only one thing worst than having the runs while flying, and that was to be a newbie with the runs. He was out flying in the AO when the diarrhea hit him. You can guess what happened—he filled his pants. Of course, since he was a newbie, his crew claimed that the combat flying scared the shit right out of him. Thank goodness Terry had a good sense of humor, but it took quite some time before they let him live it down.

When you were new, your flying did not improve as fast as you would have liked it to. One reason was that you were flying with a different AC every day, and they all flew differently. One day you would fly with an AC who wanted you to shoot your approaches steep and slow, and the next day you would fly with a guy who wanted you to shoot your approaches fast and low. As a copilot, it was hard to develop your own technique of flying. When they first flew with you, many of the ACs would only let you fly straight and level. They would shoot all the approaches until they had flown with you several times and could determine your ability. The one good thing that I liked about flying with different guys daily was that I was able to distinguish between the good pilots and the not-so-good pilots. After flying with all types of ACs, I decided that when I made AC, I would let the new guys fly as much as I could and not allow any harassment on board my aircraft.

CHAPTER 4

MY CHERRY

I truly believe that until someone has been away from their loved ones, especially in a war zone, they cannot fully understand the importance of a note or letter from home. The letters that we received were lifelines to our other world, and that world kept fading further and further into the recesses of our mind as our tour rolled along.

I wrote my mother about every two weeks. I would not tell her about the action that I was participating in, because I did not want to cause her additional worry. During my tour my Mom sent me a subscription to the *Minneapolis Star and Tribune* Sunday paper, a great gift that kept me informed of events taking place back in the States.

My two best friends from high school each wrote me once. That was the extent of their communication. Another friend of mine, Steve Djerf, wrote me weekly. I will always be grateful to him for those letters.

May 1970

Dear Mother,

Yesterday, I flew all day and night and only had four hours of sleep the night before, so I was just dead. I've already flown twenty-four hours. I guess they are averaging one hundred and forty hours in each thirty-day period. I'm learning a lot more about the War and Vietnam. I'm sure glad that none of the other kids will have to come over here. I wonder why I'm over here, in this strange country spending a whole year of my life risking even death for something I had nothing to do with.

I would like to know why? Then I look around here and then I can kind of understand because the Vietnamese are human beings in need of help and I guess that's why? I think the worst thing about being here is being away from home.

The way they are fighting this war is really stupid. We protect our enemy. If they would fight the war to win, I think it would be over a lot sooner. I just wish that all the protesters could be over here for a while; it might change their minds.

It was mid-June, and I had actively been flying in the combat zone for approximately four weeks. I had yet to receive any hits to my aircraft. That would soon change, though I had no way of knowing when. The first time that a pilot received hits to his bird was known as his "cherry." The term derived from the expression "to bust your cherry," meaning to lose your virginity. The new pilots who had not yet received any hits were considered virgins to combat or "cherry."

Have you ever been told to do something that you did not want to do but after doing it, you were glad that you did? That was exactly what happened to me, and I am extremely grateful that I did what I was told to do. When I was learning to fly back in the United States, we were taught to fly with our seat in the high position for two reasons. First, the high seat position gave you better visibility, allowing you to see over the instrument panel. Second, this high position allowed you to rest your right arm on your right thigh. Doing so gave your arm more stability for controlling the cyclic, which is the control stick—situated between your legs—used to send control movements to the rotor head. In Vietnam, however, a high seat position was very dangerous because it exposed more of your body to the enemy.

Contrary to what a lot of people thought, the Huey did not have armor. That would be impractical due to the weight of the armor. The only type of armor that the Huey had was armored pilots' seats. The seat protected your back, your bottom, and part of your left side for the AC and right side if you were a copilot. The crews also carried what we called chicken boards. A chicken board was an armored plate, approximately one inch thick, which fit into a vest you could strap onto your chest. It weighed approximately fifteen pounds and could not be worn all day—it would wear you and your back out. I usually flew without it and only tucked it under my shoulder harness straps when the fighting became intense. Other than the armor seat and the chicken board, we were quite naked. Therefore, any exposure to the enemy was dangerous.

From my first day of flying, most of the pilots I flew with advised me that I should lower my seat. I resisted doing so because lowering my seat would change the position of my body to the controls. This new position would make my flying even more uncomfortable. Being new, it was hard enough trying to learn to fly under the unfamiliar conditions of heavy gross weights and strong winds, much less having to deal with a new seat position. One day I was flying copilot with WO McCarragher, and he told me to lower my seat. I told him, "No thanks." Well, that was not going to work with McCarragher. He ordered me to drop my seat—I needed to learn to fly with the seat in the down position. At that point, I realized that I did not have any choice, so I lowered my seat. As expected, it was very uncomfortable and different to fly in this new position. With the seat all the way down, my sight picture, which I had developed for shooting approaches, was altered, and my body's relationship to the controls was different. I spent the rest of the day trying to adjust to flying with the seat down.

The next morning when I reported to the aircraft, I climbed in and thought about raising the seat back up but decided to drop it down and try it again. It was a typical morning. We lifted off from our flight line and departed north, heading towards the unit that we were assigned to for the day. We met with the unit commander and he briefed us on our mission to insert and extract troops from different locations throughout his area of operations. It was midmorning, and we were busy dropping infantry troops into a LZ when we started taking fire. We had just finished unloading the troops and were starting our liftoff out of the LZ when I looked out the windshield and saw him. Charlie (a slang word used for the enemy taken from the Army phonetic alphabet Victor Charlie for VC or Viet Cong), was standing along the perimeter of the LZ right in front of our aircraft. I watched as Charlie raised his rifle and took aim directly at me and fired. He was twenty yards in front of us, and we were at an altitude of about twenty feet when he fired. His shot entered the aircraft through the nose bubble, hitting and deflecting off my altimeter, which was situated directly in front of me about chest high. The bullet then ricocheted up, deflected off the windshield wiper and lodged about one inch above my head in the bulkhead. If I had been flying with the seat up, as I had always done before, I would have taken a direct hit right into my forehead. A second round came up through the floor and missed hitting our gunner's leg by about a half-inch. A third round struck the helicopter, hitting the fuel cell. Thank goodness the fuel did not explode. The crew chief yelled over the intercom, "We've been hit! We're leaking fuel! It's everywhere!" I snapped my head around to look, and I could see fuel running all over the cargo compartment. The AC radioed to the high ship, a helicopter that is assigned to rescue downed crews, that we were going down. He picked out an open clearing and headed for it. If that fuel ignited, we would be goners. We would be celebrating the Fourth of July a few weeks early, and we would be the grand finale.

As we set our damaged bird down in the field, our high ship hovered down beside us. Within seconds, the AC shut our bird down. We grabbed our equipment and guns, ran over, and climbed into the high ship. As soon as our entire crew was on board, the high ship took off, and we headed back to our company's flight line to pick up another bird, so that we could continue our mission. Operations would have to send Snakedoctor out to repair our bird. Snakedoctor was the call sign of our maintenance bird that flew out into the field to help fix the unflyable birds. Sometimes they would have to sling-load the damaged bird under another helicopter to get it back to our maintenance facilities. Other times they would fly Snakedoctor out into the field to fix the bird, depending upon how secure the area was and the severity of the damage to the Huey. This had been a lucky morning for us; two close calls, but no one was hurt.

This had been my cherry. It was the first time that I had taken hits in the aircraft. I had always wondered how I would react when the real shooting started. Would I be brave? Would I be scared? Would I be a hero? Or worse of all, would I be a coward? The funny thing was, I was none. It happened so fast that we just did our job and continued on our mission. My first thoughts were why did Charlie shoot at me? I had not been shooting at him. Until now, the war had not seemed personal or real to me, but now it was starting to change. I felt as if I had not been hurting anyone, yet the realization that this guy was trying to kill me disturbed me. It made me wake up and realize it did not make any difference who I was or how I felt about the war. It was very simple. I was their enemy and their job was to kill me! Later that night, as I rested in my bunk, I kept thinking about what would have happened if I had raised my seat back up as I had always done in the past. Thank goodness for McCarragher.

Your first experience is the one that leaves the biggest impression on you. The first time I saw a mutilated body was when we were flying support for an infantry unit. They had been engaged in an intense firefight and had taken heavy casualties. They were using us to transport the dead bodies back to Graves Registration, a term used for the morgue. While the infantry soldiers were loading the body bags into the back of our helicopter, one of the body bags ripped open. Out of the ripped body bag rolled the partial remains of a man. All that was left of this man's body was from his waist up. His bottom half had been blown entirely off, and the remainder of his body was so swollen and infected, it was hardly recognizable as a human being. His flesh was charcoal black, having been badly burned, and was so swollen that it was twice the size of a normal person. The smell was even worse than the sight. I just sat there and stared. I had never seen anything like this before. If I had seen this back in the States, I would have gotten sick and probably vomited. But not now—I was becoming conditioned to the war.

Several times when we carried dead bodies, the crew chief and gunner would wear their gas masks, because they were situated downwind and the smell was so terrible that it would make them vomit. There were other times when they were not lucky enough to have their gas masks with them. It was during these times that I would not have traded places with our crew for anything. Whenever we finished carrying dead bodies, we always tried to fly back to a place where we could wash the inside of the aircraft, to remove the risk of infecting the food and the supplies we would be carrying later.

During my first few months in country, our company did not experience a lot of intense action. This lack of heavy combat made for a better learning environment. My flying was improving, and I was starting to get a good feel for the aircraft. I was also starting to understand how our operations worked, and I was getting to know the pilots on an individual basis.

Our missions consisted of flying resupply for the different ground units in the brigade that the 71st AHC supported. We also flew combat assaults and eagle flights. A combat assault consisted of forming a group of helicopters and loading them with infantry troops. We would launch an attack against the enemy, using the helicopter to carry the troops right into the action. This helicopter assault was very similar to the cavalry attacks back in the West, except we were using the helicopter rather than the horse. An eagle flight was using the helicopter much like an eagle, soaring over the ground for observation.

I personally liked flying resupply missions the best. This was because we would get to execute what we called a high overhead approach, which I loved to do. When we flew resupply, we would first fly to the support base to load our aircraft with supplies and then head out to the unit's AO that we were supporting. We would locate the troops out in the field by using maps and grid coordinates. When we thought that we had located the proper coordinates, we would call the unit on the radio. "Charlie Platoon, this is Rattler One-Seven, over." "Roger Rattler One-Seven, we have you in sight." Once we raised radio contact, we would ask the unit to pop smoke. "Charlie Platoon, this is Rattler One-Seven, pop smoke." The ground unit would throw out a smoke grenade. We would look and identify the color. "Charlie Platoon, we have a red smoke over." "Roger, Rattler One-Seven, we confirm a red smoke," the ground unit would reply.

We would always get the unit on the ground to pop a smoke before going into the LZ for two reasons. First, we needed to know the direction of the wind. It was very important in flying a helicopter that you made your approach into the wind. An approach downwind, especially in a heavy chopper, could be disastrous due to the aerodynamic relationship of lift and angle of attack as it applied to the relative wind. Second, we had to identify and verify that we were at the right location for the right ground unit. Therefore, we always asked the unit that we were supporting to pop smoke.

Many times we would see two or three smokes after making the call. Charlie would be monitoring our frequency and throw out a couple of smokes, hoping that we would head for the first smoke that we saw without first identifying its color, thus setting us up to fly into an ambush. That was why we came back with the color first. Then we would have the unit on the ground confirm if our color was correct or not. Several times we would see two of the same color smokes. We then would have our unit throw out another smoke, and we would try for another identification of the proper color. Every so often a soldier on the ground would pop a smoke and say, "I've thrown a red smoke," thus compromising the color. Then every smoke that we would see would be red. When this happened, we would tell him to pop another smoke, but not to mention the color. "We'll call the color and you verify it." We had a bird in our sister company, the Dolphins, that got shot down because they did not properly identify the color of the smoke. They shot an approach to the wrong smoke, and Charlie was on the ground waiting for them. It was the perfect ambush.

After we confirmed the color of the smoke, we would fly over the LZ so that the wind was 90 degrees off the left side of the nose of our aircraft, at an altitude of about 2500 feet. This altitude allowed for a good margin of safety from small arms fire. When we were directly over the LZ, we would lower the collective and roll the bird into a steep left turn. This would set up the helicopter in a steep descending turn. Our rate of descent would be between two and three thousand feet per minute as we made our 450 degree turn. Within seconds of starting the approach, we would begin our roll out and be established on short final to the LZ. All we had to do was flair the helicopter while adding power, and within seconds we would be hovering in the LZ. The benefits of this kind of approach was that it took a minimum amount of time to get into the LZ, and if we did take a hit while making our approach, we would just continue down and land in the LZ where friendly troops were located. I enjoyed executing this maneuver more than any other aspect of our flying. With the high number of overhead approaches that we were able to shoot, we became really good at them—plus it was just plain fun, almost as fun as a good amusement park ride. Many of the pilots would do 360 degrees high overheads, but I liked the 450 better. The one bad aspect of flying resupply was that normally we would be flying single ship, and when flying single ship, if you had an emergency or were shot down, there was no one in proximity to rescue you.

Flying combat assaults was an entirely different type of flying from resupply. We would fly first to the staging area to join up with a number of other birds. The ACs would get together for a briefing of the assault that we were getting ready to insert. The briefing would consist of the name of the unit that we would be supporting, the time of the assault, and the number of sorties that we would be expected to do. They would also brief the location and coordinates of the assault and the security, or lack of it, in the LZ.

After the briefing we would assemble the helicopters in formation. The size of the LZ would dictate how many birds could be put in each formation and what type it would be. We would be assigned our position in the flight with a chalk number. Normally a senior aircraft commander (SAC) would lead the flight. A SAC was an aircraft commander who had been AC for at least three months without any accidents. The other SACs had chosen him because he was a good stick and had the ability to lead. Not everyone made SAC; it was considered an honor to be chosen. I immediately picked SAC as my goal.

After obtaining a chalk number, we were assigned a radio frequency for all calls. A typical monitoring of the frequency would sound like, "Flight, this is Chalk One, who's up?" "Chalk Two's up." "Chalk Three's up." "Chalk Four's up." "Chalk Five's up." "OK flight, we'll be lifting in three seconds." The lead ship would lift off and the formation would depart from the staging area, headed for the pickup zone (PZ). The flight would transition to the designated PZ, where we would pick up our infantry troops. We would normally carry six soldiers with full gear per bird. After we finished loading the troops into the aircraft, the flight lead would depart with the other aircraft following in formation. Our destination was the LZ, where the combat assault would take place.

While we were busy loading the troops, the mission commander, who was another SAC, was out scouting the LZ. After the mission commander located the LZ, he would first fly a high recon of the area to determine what would be the safest and best approach and departure routes. He would consider the direction of the wind, the locations and movement of the enemy troops, and the terrain and any obstacles. After he decided on the best approach and departure paths, his next duty was to mark the LZ with a smoke. He could do this himself, by flying down over the LZ and throwing out a smoke grenade, or he could get another aircraft to mark it for him. Once the LZ was marked, it was time for the gunships to do their work. They would fly in low, prepping the LZ with rockets and minigun fire to ensure that any enemy soldiers hiding in the LZ would be dead by the time the slicks arrived.

In our area of operation was a remnant of a LZ, where a flight of three ships flew in without first prepping the LZ. Charlie was dug into the LZ waiting for them. On short final, Charlie popped out of his hole and ambushed the aircraft. All three helicopters crashed and burned on the spot. During my first week in Vietnam, one of the ACs flew me over this LZ. I could still see the remains of the crashed aircraft on the ground in perfect formation. I will always remember my AC telling me, "This is what happens when you don't prep the LZ." Seeing the remains of the crashed aircraft on the ground definitely instilled in me the necessity of always prepping an unsecured LZ. As they say, one look is worth a thousand words.

Once our gunships were done prepping the LZ, the lead ship would begin its descent with the other birds following in formation. Our door gunners would be firing their M60 machine guns, while our gunships made gun runs alongside the formation, laying down fire, as we descended into the LZ. The main mission of the first group of soldiers dropped into the LZ was to secure the perimeter and keep it secured for the rest of the assault. The combat assault was a quick and efficient way to mobilize the infantry.

Flying formation was more strenuous than flying resupply, because you were flying in close proximity of other aircraft. The distance we flew from the bird in front of us ranged from as close as two feet to eight feet. When you were flying this close to another bird, you had to be very alert and on top of your game. A slight distraction would be fatal. I quickly learned who I could fly close to and who I had better keep a few extra feet from, to allow for their flying technique. Any quick control movements made while flying in a close formation could be disastrous. You had to put great faith in the guy flying the bird in front of you.

In our company, we normally flew in three types of formations: trail formation, echelon right, and echelon left. Trail formation was formed by lining up the aircraft, one behind the other, in a straight line. The second bird would fly slightly above the first, and the third above the second, and so on. For an observer on the ground, the trail formation would look like a straight line with each aircraft flying slightly above the one he is formed up on. On the other hand, an echelon right formation was when the birds lined up in a parallel line each to the right of the one in its front, so that the whole had an appearance of steps. Again, each bird flew slightly above the one in its front. Finally, an echelon left was the same except the birds would form to the left of the bird in their front.

Another form of flying that I learned when I was new in country was low-level flying. In the 71st AHC we had a company policy: if you could not maintain an altitude of at least 1500 feet due to the low cloud ceiling, you were required to fly low-level. The theory was that the less time you were exposed to the enemy's line of fire, the greater the margin of safety you had from being shot down. The army found the helicopter in combat had two very dangerous disadvantages: it was very noisy, thus broadcasting to the enemy that you were coming; and it was very slow. In low-level flight, you learned to conceal both of these disadvantages. For example, if Charlie was standing in a small clearing and you were flying treetop level at 110 knots, he would not hear you until you were literally on top of him. By the time it took him to raise his rifle and take a shot, you were gone from the clearing.

When flying low-level, we always tried to stay over the trees rather than fly along the tree lines. We also tried to fly perpendicular to the tree lines rather than parallel to them because if Charlie were standing along the tree line, it gave him a better chance of getting a bead on us. Low-level flying was exciting, but also very dangerous, because pilots often flew too low and ended up hitting trees. Your reflexes and response times had to be very quick when flying within inches of the trees—the slightest wrong control movement would be disastrous. Many pilots in our company cracked nose bubbles against tree-tops while flying low-level. It was not uncommon after landing for the crew chief to hop out and clear the tree branches from the skids.

One morning, I was assigned to an early mission that included a pickup before the sun came up. The mission started with a pickup from a helicopter pad located down the beach from our company area. I was assigned to fly with an AC whom I had flown with before. He was usually quite a good pilot, but not that morning. The night before, he had been up drinking till 0200 hours, and he was not sober or alert enough to be flying. But there he was. It was a simple, straight-in approach to the helicopter pad with no obstacles in our approach path. On his first approach, he was way too high and fast. He whizzed right past the pad. He circled around and said, "I'll try it again." He tried another approach, and to my amazement and amusement, he missed the pad again. At this point I offered to take the aircraft controls. I shot the next approach and set the chopper down on the pad. I thought to myself, "This could be a long day, if he can't even shoot a simple approach to an open pad, how is he going to function in the AO?" Luckily for us, it was an easy morning. He let me do most the flying while he sobered up. It was hard enough to fly sober, but flying drunk? That was crazy in my book.

I learned early in my tour that a lot of the soldiers acted differently over in Nam than at home. Vietnam was so different that many of the soldiers felt that the moral values they learned when growing up did not apply over here. It was as if they were living a different life, and they would not be held responsible for their behavior. I knew many soldiers that felt the South Vietnamese were just Vietnamese and not allies. They did not classify them or think of them as human beings; therefore, they did not have to treat them as such. Once, while we were returning to Chu Lai at the end of the day, I heard an explosion directly below our bird. The gunner had thrown out a grenade into some friendly hootchs that we were flying over, just for kicks. I looked over at the AC and it did not seem to bother him a bit. I decided right then and there that when I made AC, I would keep strict control over my crew. On questioning the gunner, he told me that he did not see anything wrong with what he was doing, because they were just Vietnamese. To kill in battle was one thing, but to kill for enjoyment was sick, I thought.

To some of the guys, I think this type of thought and action was a form of rebellion. Those types of guys would shoot anything that moved—women, kids, it did not matter, as long as the AC let them. As a Huey AC flying in our AO, the only person who could police our actions was our commander, or our own conscience. Much of what I saw and experienced as a copilot helped me to set my standards for when I made AC.

Every aviation unit had their own way of picking their aircraft commanders. In the 71st, the ACs voted on the copilots who they thought were ready to make AC. Only by unanimous decision would a copilot get picked to make AC. Personally, I did not think this was the fairest way, for one AC could hold a copilot back from making AC for personal reasons rather than for his flying ability, and at times this happened. The normal time to make AC ranged from four to five months, depending on the individual's ability or the need to make new ACs because of the old ones going home. Making AC was a major turning point in your tour, for then you could make your own decisions. You could fly the way you thought best, rather than trying to please the AC you were flying with that particular day. Another nice advantage was that your unit accepted you and respected you as an AC, whereas as a copilot, you were just another newbie.

Sex was another issue that really blew my mind as a newbie. Not that I did not know about sex, but it was the way that many of our married men behaved regarding it. The single men's behavior was kind of expected, but of the men who had wives and children back home, I had expected most would play it straight. I found out that it was unusual for married men not to fool around with the hookers. I had been raised in a nice lower-middle-class neighborhood where all the young married men would play ball with us teenagers. Growing up, we got to know them fairly well and they were all pretty straight when it came to women and the subject of fooling around on their wives. Being young and probably naïve, I just figured that most married men were the same.

One night, during one of the frequent drinking parties, the pilots brought in a Vietnamese whore. She was fourteen at the oldest, probably more like twelve or thirteen. Sure enough, more than half of the pilots there that night were lined up for that little girl. Now, right in the middle of the line stood one of our commanding officers. I guess he was showing his good example of leadership. There were more married guys than singles in that line. I personally could not imagine being the 29th or 30th person to have sex with that little girl.

We would talk to these guys about their wives and families. When asked what they would do if they caught their wife sleeping around, their common response was either beating her, divorcing her, or worse, maybe killing her. Yet, these same guys thought it was all right

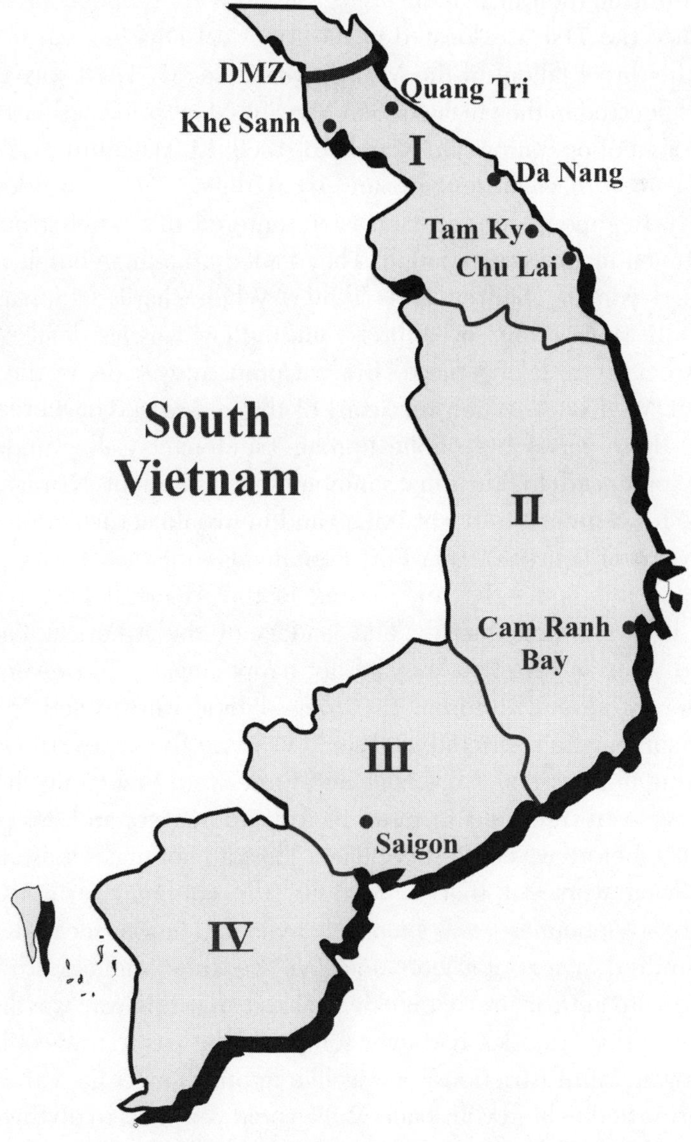

4. Map of South Vietnam. The country was divided into four corps tactical zones.

for them to cheat, a typical double standard. One of the biggest jokes over in Vietnam was for a guy to go to Hawaii on his R&R (rest and relaxation) and catch the clap from his wife. I never personally knew anyone to which this happened, but I can imagine a lot of the wives caught it from their husbands.

Since the 71st was located in the Americal Division, we suffered from the direct fallout of the My Lai Massacre. My Lai 4 was a small hamlet, located in the village of Son My. Son My was located just south of our area of operation. On March 16, 1968, Lt. William L. Calley Jr. and the men of Charlie Company, 1st Battalion, 11th Brigade, 20th Infantry Regiment, Americal Division, entered this rebel stronghold expecting a major confrontation. They ended up lashing out at mostly unarmed women, children, and old men. When Charlie Company was done with their killing, over three hundred civilians lay dead.[5] While this atrocity was taking place, Bravo Company was doing the same thing at My Khe 4. When the word of this massacre got back to the States, there was a big public uproar. Lieutenant Calley ended up being sentenced to life imprisonment, but President Nixon would reduce his sentence to twenty years and he would actually only serve three years of house arrest at Fort Benning, Georgia.[6]

Since the 71st AHC was located in the Americal Division, this made it even worse for us. The leaders of the Americal Division wanted to make sure that this did not happen again. To prevent this, they set up several different fire zones. Some were called free-fire zones, some were restricted, and some were no-fire zones. If we were operating in a restricted fire zone and there were Viet Cong shooting at us, we were required to radio in to headquarters and get proper clearance before we could shoot back. This did not make sense to me. Then even worse, if that same dink (the common term used to describe a Vietnamese) was shooting at you and he was located within five hundred meters of a Vietnamese village, they would not give you clearance to return fire. I quickly realized that this war was like no other war that America had ever fought in the past. How could you fight a war with restrictions? It was like fighting someone with one of your arms tied behind your back. Why would you want to do this? This was not like the John Wayne movies that I had watched growing up.

As the days passed into months, my sensitivities hardened, and I became emotionally colder. I learned not to allow the harsh things that I was experiencing to emotionally affect me. During those first months, I became quite close with WO Garrett. Garrett was always talking about why were we over here fighting the war. This was a question that I had never thought much about myself, especially before arriving in Vietnam. Garrett was always trying to justify the war, and he could not. This really bothered him. It was hard to justify any war, much less a war that you were not fighting to win. The many talks that I had with Garrett made me think about what I was doing. I actually did not know if this was a smart thing to do in a war zone. Garrett and his many questions were partially responsible for me deciding that I did not want to fly guns. I thought about what Israel had told me on my first day of flying, that he did not think I would want to be a gunship pilot after being here a couple of weeks and seeing their mission and the flying that they did. I had thought that flying guns would be a blast, being able to shoot all the rockets and missiles just like in the shows I had watched while growing up. But after talking to Garrett, I was asking myself, "Did I really want to do this type of flying?" Most of the gunship pilots appeared to enjoy the killing and the fun of blowing things away. After a lot of thought, I realized that flying guns was not for me. I would fight when called upon to do so, but I really did not enjoy it. There were many times during my tour that the gunship pilots saved my life, and I will always be thankful to them, but their way was not for me.

Garrett once wrote a letter to President Nixon, asking to be sent home. I was really surprised when a few weeks later he received a reply. I thought it was nice of the White House to answer, but apparently they did not see things in the same light as Garrett, for he spent the rest of his tour alongside us in the 71st. Garrett was one of the few pilots in our company that I held in high regard. He had great love for his wife and child and was always talking about them, and I respected that. For myself, I found out that the more I thought about home, the harder it was, and so I put those thoughts out of my mind. I realized that writing letters home always depressed me, so I wrote as few as possible. When I did write home, they were usually short notes to tell either my girlfriend or family that I was ok. When I had been stationed at Fort Carson, Colorado, one of the ex-Vietnam pilots had told me, "Vietnam was hell, not just the war, but just being there." I was beginning to understand what he meant. It was the small things that we missed that made us feel that way. Not being able to go out with your girl, not being able to get a hamburger, a slice of pizza, or just go out on a walk in the countryside by yourself. I began to realize how much these small things meant to me and how much I took them for granted.

CHAPTER 5

SPECIAL OPERATIONS

July 15, 1970

Dear Jim,

Well, I received your letter today. Tell mother that I'm sorry that I hadn't written sooner, but for the last seven days I was real sick. The sickest that I can ever remember. This is just no place to get sick because you can't take care of yourself and no one else will. A couple of days I was so weak I could hardly walk. I went six days without eating because I couldn't get a hold of anything. It's the worse I ever was in my whole life. I'm still grounded, but feel a lot better. I'll go to the flight surgeon and get cleared for flight tomorrow. I'm feeling down in the dumps. People act so different over here, its really sad. They let their morals drop. They act like a bunch of kids.

All I do is try to analyze what I see about this war. The way we spend our money, time, etc. and how we are taken for granted. How no one appreciates what we are doing here, except maybe the ARVN forces. I just can't see going out risking my life for no reason, except to maintain the same situation that we have been in for the last six years. I guess I'm just for fighting a war if I'm going to fight it and not be a part of a political circus. I thought I would really enjoy flying over here, because you would get the self satisfaction of helping people, but you can't get that satisfaction. The worst thing is that we don't know why we are here. I sure wish that I did. It sure would make this year go so much easier.

I'm kind of looking for the monsoons, so it will cool off. I just don't dig this heat. Please excuse my handwriting, but I'm tired. Well, take care and say hi to everyone for me.

As June rolled into July, my tour was going along smoothly. I was kept busy learning the physical aspects of flying a helicopter in combat. I was also developing a good understanding of mission operations. At the beginning of July, our unit was assigned a "Special Operations" mission of flying and supporting the MACV-SOG, CCN. MACV stood for Military Assistance Command Vietnam and the SOG stood for Studies and Observation Group. This was actually a covert name for secret teams that performed deep penetration missions of strategic reconnaissance and interdiction. CCN stood for Command and Control North. They were an organization assigned under the 5th Special Forces Group that directed the operations in the northern areas of Vietnam and especially Laos.

Due to the nature of the mission and with whom we would be working, this special mission was entirely voluntary for our flight crews. Still being quite new and eager for excitement, I, along with several other Rattler pilots, volunteered for the mission. On the first day of our special assignment we were given orders to report to a specific area located on the Chu Lai airfield. This area housed some old air force revetments no longer in use. The SOG team had chosen this area for their command post and had separated and secured it from the rest of the airfield. No one was allowed in or out of this area without special permission. It was at this location that we received our first briefing from the SOG team. Our mission would consist of inserting and extracting SOG teams into Laos, who would then monitor North Vietnamese Army (NVA) movements along the Ho Chi Minh Trail. Some of the team members would infiltrate the NVA troops with the hope of locating prisoner of war (POW) camps. We would be working with the CCN people and the Army of the Republic of Vietnam (ARVN) Special Forces.

The CCN soldiers were mostly U.S. Special Forces (Green Berets), with some Navy Seals and Air Force Combat Controllers also assigned to this secret, unconventional warfare task force. We were told during our briefing that if we revealed any information about these missions, we would be liable for up to ten years imprisonment and a ten thousand dollar fine. The scariest part was that we were also told if we were unfortunate enough to be shot down or captured while performing these missions, our government would deny having any involvement or that we even existed because the United States was still denying publicly that we had any military involvement in Laos. Since I was so young, this came as a surprise to me. This was the first time that I realized the government was actually doing things behind its citizens' backs and publicly claiming that they were not.

The American special ops troops seemed very professional and appeared to be experts at what they were doing. Unlike the regular ARVN soldiers, the ARVN Special Forces seemed very dedicated to their cause. I was impressed with their professionalism and especially their rappelling skills.

All of our mission insertions and extractions would take place in Laos. The first time I flew into Laos, I felt as if my security blanket had been ripped away from my shoulders. My security of being familiar with our area of operations was gone. The thought of being shot down this far inland made me realize that our crew would have to beat our way through the jungle for days just to get back into Vietnam. Once back, we would still be in the western part of the country, far from most of our troops located near the coast, so we would have to travel for several more days and avoid being spotted by the NVA. I always felt that the coastline offered us safety—if we could make it to the coast, we would always be able to locate and reunite with friendly troops.

One of the first things that grabbed my attention when flying over Laos was the banana groves. What amazed me even more was that these banana groves that seemed to be the middle of nowhere had fences around them and no one else around. It had to be Charlie growing them.

Most of the terrain that we flew over in Laos consisted of a double canopy forest. Underneath was the Ho Chi Minh Trail, a dirt road that had been cut out of the jungle and as wide in some areas as a four-lane highway. We never spotted any movement during the day on this road, but at night we knew this trail was as busy as the roads back home. Seeing for myself the immenseness of the Ho Chi Minh Trail gave me a good understanding of how the NVA could move their supplies down from the North to the South so easily.

Our mission was to insert ARVN Special Forces teams into Laos. These teams normally consisted of one American operative and six or seven ARVN Special Forces soldiers. Due to the denseness of the jungle canopy, we would normally use a ladder or a jungle penetrator, which was hung from the bottom of our helicopter, to make the insertion. Once we inserted the team, we would return to our staging field and wait. The insertion team would try to set up an observation point along the Ho Chi Minh Trail to monitor the movements of the NVA and follow up on any leads that they had received prior to starting their mission. When we inserted the team, the ARVN Special Forces were dressed like the enemy. Some of the ARVN Special Forces would actually try to infiltrate the enemy troops and seek out information. I thought that took a lot of balls! If we were called after insertion, it was almost always because the enemy had discovered them, and once discovered, the team had no other alternative if they wanted to survive but to be extracted. This made our mission of extraction very dangerous—the enemy would be in close proximity to the team and be looking for us to come rescue them. So much for the element of surprise.

One night while we were on standby, we received a call for a night extraction. One of the SOG teams had been discovered by the NVA and was surrounded. They felt they could not make it until daylight, and their only chance for survival was to be pulled out immediately. It would be up to us to save them. I was assigned to fly with AC Kerry McMahon, who had come to Vietnam in 1969 and was one of our most experienced pilots. His call sign was Rattler 19. McMahon was slight in both build and height, probably no more than 140 pounds. Everyone in our unit called him Little Mac. I had flown with Little Mac quite a bit since arriving in Nam, and in my opinion he was the best stick in our unit. I was glad to be flying with him for such a tough extraction.

After completing our briefing, we cranked up our bird and headed west towards Laos. It was one of those dark, lonely nights without even a sliver of the moon to light up the sky. When we were within radio range of the CCN team on the ground, Little Mac keyed his mike, shattering the radio silence and giving the team a call. Their response

5. Warrant Officer first, then Lieutenant Kerry McMahon. Everyone called him Little Mac. He was the best of the best. (Photo courtesy of Don Lynam.)

came back across our radio in a soft whisper. Their voices echoed the near panic that we knew they felt. I could feel the hairs on the back of my neck stand straight up as I sat there listening to their quivering voices, knowing that we were going to fly right down into the middle of their mess. With no city lights to reflect off the clouds, it was extremely dark over the countryside of Laos when we located the team's position. We were going to have to shoot a nighttime approach to a soldier holding a strobe light. But what really made this tricky was that he was standing down in a little clearing, in the dense, dark, jungle, surrounded by the enemy. The battery-operated strobe light that he held was approximately six inches high and three inches wide, not a lot of light to find in the darkness of the night, in the middle of Laos.

When we located the team, they were situated up in a wooded hollow surrounded by hills on three sides. As we flew closer, Little Mac radioed the unit to turn on their strobe light. Once we located the strobe, he quickly swung the chopper around and set her up on final approach. As he lowered the collective and descended the helicopter below the ridgelines, it became so dark in our cockpit that the tree lines were hidden from view. It was like descending into nothingness. We had been entirely blacked out on our approach up to this point. We had all our external lights off. Our instrument lights were as low as we could set them and still be able to read them. As we descended lower, we found ourselves located in the middle of a black hole at a hover. With our eyes adjusted to the darkness, we still were unable to see anything, much less locate the troops. Little Mac did the only thing that he could—he flipped on our landing light. We went instantly from total darkness to blinding lightness. I suddenly felt like a big plump turkey at a turkey shoot, sitting there with our landing light on, surrounded by the enemy.

We quickly located the team and hovered our ship towards them, cutting our way through the dense foliage. The PZ was so small and tight that we were literally chopping our way through tree limbs. We could hear, "Whack, whack, whack," from the rotor blades as Little Mac maneuvered the bird towards the PZ. He lowered the bird down as the team rushed towards us. It seemed like we hovered for hours while the team climbed aboard. I was waiting for the shell to hit that would send us crashing to the ground, but to my amazement we did not even draw fire. As the last ARVN soldier climbed on board, Little Mac nudged the cyclic forward and pulled pitch. Slowly our chopper edged forward as we searched the horizon for the opening, which would take us through the trees and lead us to safety. Slowly but surely, we climbed for the altitude that would give us refuge from the enemy below. The whole approach had taken less than a few minutes, but what a few minutes. Little Mac had performed some of the best flying that I had ever seen. Right then, I set my goal to be just as good a pilot. When we returned to our staging area, we received many thanks from the team that we pulled out. It made us feel good to know that these guys greatly appreciated us.

During the days we were flying these special missions, the rest of our company had been supporting our regular brigade in the local area. Then our unit received orders for a new campaign, to fly support for the 2nd ARVN Infantry Division and the 6th ARVN Regiment.

(The Vietnamese name was DT.639/QT.63B. DT stood for Dong Tien, which means Advance Together, and QT stood for Quyet Thang, which means Resolved to Win.) The division's orders were to advance west from Da Nang to an old abandoned airfield called Kham Duc, located due west of our area of operations in western Vietnam. American forces had been to Kham Duc before and had received heavy losses when pulling out. The plan was to occupy Kham Duc and stage search-and-destroy missions into the enemy territory. The campaign would run from July 12 until September 4, allowing our troops to pull out before the monsoons began. The ARVN would be using their infantry troops with our helicopters for transportation and support.

Reconnaissance revealed a lot of enemy activity in this area. The first assignment was to secure the old abandoned airstrip. Our orders were to insert the infantry troops onto the airstrip. In our briefing, we were told to expect a lot of enemy contact on our initial insertion, but to our surprise the insertion went smoothly, with only light contact with the enemy. It did not take long before the ARVN troops had the old airstrip secured. Once the troops we inserted had the perimeter of the airfield secured, the commander called in the CH-47 Chinooks. The Chinooks were twin rotor, heavy lift helicopters built by Boeing. They had two engines; if one failed, the other engine could run both rotors. It also had a synchronization unit that kept the intermeshing rotor blades clear of each other. The Chinooks were used to haul in the artillery and the heavy equipment to the ARVN, in an effort to establish a strong outpost at Kham Duc. Most of our company's flying would be based out of there for the next five weeks. Kham Duc would also be a good refueling point for the special missions that we were flying, due to its close proximity to Laos.

July 21, 1970

Dear Mother,

In Jim's letter, he wrote and asked what kind of flying I do. Well, I'm a slick pilot. Lately most of the flying has been combat assaults, carrying troops. The last few weeks we've been way up in the mountains, about five clicks from Laos. The terrain is really bad and it takes all the flying skills you have to fly into the LZs. They are small, tight and most of the times there's so many trees and stumps that you can't set down. You just have to hover while the troops jump out. Been flying a lot of ARVN troops. It's hot and the winds are strong. It's real easy to lose your RPM and that's bad, because when your engine and rotor RPM start going down, if you can't hold it, you're going to crash. It's so much tougher than the pilots flying down south in the Delta. At least, I will be a lot better pilot flying in the mountains. If we're not flying CA's, we're flying resupply for the troops, all through our area of operations, which is basically the U.S. 196th Inf. Brigade and the 6th ARVN Brigade.

I sure will be glad to get back to the states. I guess I still have a long wait. It's so easy to get over tired over here. I just rest every moment I get.

As the days passed by, I alternated my flying between the special mission and our unit's regular flying out of Kham Duc. One day I was assigned a mission to defoliate the immediate area around the old airstrip. Early that morning, our ground crew rigged our ship with spray booms, a chemical sprayer, and tank. When I looked at our bird, I thought to myself, "What a mean looking crop duster!" It was the coolest thing I had ever seen. We would be spraying a chemical called Orange (known after the war as "Agent" Orange). When they finished rigging the aircraft, we had the chemical tank filled and took off to accomplish our spraying. Spraying defoliate was exciting and fun. We would fly right down on the treetops, just inches above the limbs, as we made passes back and forth along the perimeter. Within a week, we would fly back over the same area that we had sprayed earlier, and all the vegetation would be shriveled up and dead. This opened up the perimeters we had sprayed and made it easier for our troops to see the enemy, when and if they were going to try to sneak up on us.

After we finished spraying the perimeter, we were ordered to spray the rice paddies that were located within a few kilometers of the airstrip, presumably the enemy's food supply. During the spraying of one of these rice patties, we swung the helicopter around and dropped her down for a straight run across a patty with a scarecrow in the middle of the field. At first glance, I did not give the scarecrow another

6. Aerial view of the Kham Duc airstrip. Notice how barren the perimeter of the airstrip is after being sprayed with Agent Orange. (Photo courtesy of Don Lynam.)

thought, but as we flew closer, I realized that this particular scarecrow was holding an AK47! We immediately pulled our bird up and popped over the trees to get out of the line of sight from this gook scarecrow. We swung the bird back around to where he had been standing to get him, but he was gone and was nowhere to be found.

While we were busy spraying Agent Orange in Vietnam, back in the States there was a big stink going on about the use of defoliate spraying. I personally felt at the time that it was one of the best operations we had. It actually hurt the enemy and at the same time helped our troops. Out in this No Man's Land, we found beautifully cultivated rice paddies that Charlie would raise during the night, and when ripe, would harvest for his food supply. By spraying this rice with Agent Orange, we were helping to eliminate the enemy's food supply, thus making it more difficult for Charlie to supply their soldiers in the field. I could never understand why the people back home appeared to be always working against their own soldiers. I felt that when you fight, you should fight to win, or do not bother fighting. We were to find out years later about the devastating effects of Agent Orange on the human body, and the biggest tragedy was that it appeared our government was aware of the dangers at the time we were spraying it.

Our regular flying duties out of Kham Duc consisted mainly of search-and-destroy missions. We would insert troops into one area, and then after they had searched the area and destroyed anything they found, we would pull them out and insert them into another area. We did these missions for several days. The ARVN soldiers found many signs of enemy troops, but made little contact. They were doing a lot of searching, but very little destroying.

August 15, 1970, would be one of the worst days of my tour. I will always remember it well, for it was also my twentieth birthday. I was scheduled to fly special ops that day. One of the other copilots scheduled to fly that day was down, so they asked for volunteers. A new pilot in our unit, Lt. James Becker, volunteered for the open position. Lieutenant Becker had graduated from Sam Houston State University in 1966 and attended Brite Divinity School at Ft. Worth from 1966 to 1968. He was married and had a new baby boy. He would not live to see the end of the day.

For this special operation, we had a flight of five slick helicopters. The flight consisted of three Rattlers and two Minutemen helicopters. Flying for the three Rattlers were WO Mark Dobbs and myself, WO Andy Anderson and Lt. James Becker, and WO Les Winfield and WO Mike Kruger. Early morning on August 15 we received a call that one of the CCN teams was in trouble. The team had been in close contact with the enemy all night and was near exhaustion as they cried for help. We received a quick briefing of the situation, immediately cranked up our flight of five Hueys, and departed for Laos. We were not allowed to take any gunships, but we had an Air Force fixed-wing as our forward air controller (FAC). The FAC was a person who normally coordinated air strikes but today was coordinating our extraction.

Chalk One, or first position, was flown by a Minutemen crew whose copilot was named Lt. Joe Gross. I knew Joe from flight school.

He had already earned his commission as an officer before going to flight school, so he was not a warrant officer candidate. I got to know him pretty well since we both had the same name, just that I was Charles Joseph and he was Joseph Charles Gross.

Within a mile or so of the PZ, Chalk One started taking heavy fire, was damaged, and quickly went down. Joe and his crew steered their damaged bird towards a clearing situated up on a knoll. Milking his sick bird, he arrived and managed to make a safe landing.

We immediately broke off from the flight and headed towards the downed bird. The other Minutemen aircraft made it there first, so we continued down to give cover. Dobbs told our gunners to go hot as we swung our helicopter down to cover the rescue bird. Our M60s sang their familiar song of "Tat, tat, tat" for about fifteen seconds, and then suddenly went silent. I swung my head around to look at our crew, and both the crew chief and gunner were banging on their guns trying to get them unjammed. I could not believe both of the M60s had jammed at the same time. We were taking heavy fire but were unable to return it. The downed crew quickly exited their helicopter and ran over and jumped into the Minutemen ship. The rescue ship took a lot of fire going in but managed to get off the knoll safely. The crew was safe but we had to leave the helicopter in Laos.

WO Anderson and Lt. Becker flew Chalk Two. Spc4 Michael Crist was the crew chief and Spc4 Peter Schmidt was their gunner. Chalk Two started their descent into the PZ, which was situated on a wooded knoll running east to west with a steep embankment on the south side. Due to the rough terrain and the trees, Chalk Two used a rappelling ladder, which hung from the right side of the aircraft, to extract the troops. Anderson brought his Huey to a hover approximately fifty feet over the PZ and lowered the rapelling ladder down to the CCN team. Five team members scrambled aboard the ladder. As Anderson started his takeoff, his bird suddenly pitched down and quickly crashed into the trees, rolling to its right side and crashing down the south side of the hill. Even though we watched it, we were not sure what had happened—had the bird been shot down, did the engine quit, or had the ladder hooked on the trees? It happened so quickly. The only thing that we knew for sure was that they were taking extremely heavy fire at the time.

Meanwhile, the clouds and ceiling were rapidly lowering, and our fuel supply was running low. The Minutemen ship that had rescued the first crew had already headed back to Kham Duc, and with two aircraft shot down, that left only Winfield's ship and ours. We knew that we had to take as many troops as we could possibly lift out of the jungle, so we began our descent into the PZ, shooting our approach from the west to the east. We received heavy fire from the ground as we shot our approach. Our guns were unjammed by then, and our crew was busy returning fire. We made it into the PZ, and Dobbs hovered the chopper as the troops struggled to climb aboard. Within seconds, we had loaded and lifted off, dangerously heavy from the number of troops onboard. Our bird was feeling her pain, groaning as she edged her way upward. Several trees blocked our flight path as we tried to exit the PZ, but Dobbs precisely maneuvered the overloaded bird

7. A C-123 taxing at the Kham Duc airstrip with a Firebird Charlie model gunship parked in the background. (Photo courtesy of Don Lynam.)

between them. He kept trying to pull more pitch to clear the trees, but our rotor rpm (revolutions per minute) kept bleeding off due to our excessive weight. When your rpm bleeds off, the only thing you can do to stop from crashing is to lower the collective and reduce power.

A copilot's job in this situation is to back up the AC. I needed to crosscheck and monitor the engine instruments and call out any abnormal indications. Tracers were flying everywhere as we began our liftoff. I read out the rpm to Dobbs, as it bled down, "6500, 6400, 6300." We had no choice but to continue forward, as I reported "6200, 6100." Dobbs was maneuvering the Huey between trees, cutting branch tips as we slowly climbed from the hell below. We could hear the blades tearing through the branches as we cut our way upward. We would gain a little altitude, and then we would have to reduce the power to regain the rpm. When we lowered the power, we would start chopping the trees again. It was Dobbs's excellent piloting skills that got us out and away from the trees that wanted to engulf us. After what seemed like an eternity, we made it clear of the trees, where it was easier to climb the overloaded bird to an altitude that was safe from the small arms fire from below. As long as I live, I will never forget the expression on Dobbs's face. He had this look of sheer amazement in his eyes. Dobbs turned to me and said, "You're one of the bravest guys I've ever met or the dumbest." He could not believe that I stayed so calm with all the action taking place. I laughed and thought to myself, "I was neither, I was just doing my job."

After we climbed to safety, we headed back to Kham Duc to drop off the troops and refuel. Once we refueled, we planned to return to pick up the rest of the downed crew. By the time we returned to Kham Duc and refueled, however, CCN gave us orders to stay put. We could not believe it. We still had men needing extraction, and we wanted to go back and at least try to get a good look at Anderson's downed bird. During our earlier extraction, we had managed to pull out Crist, the crew chief from Anderson's bird. Crist told me that when he had left the crashed ship, Lt. Becker was still in the aircraft, strapped in his seat and unconscious but still alive. He also told me that their gunner, Schmidt, was pinned under the aircraft but alive as well. There were gooks everywhere, and it was complete mayhem as he scrambled up the hillside to get to our ship.

Dobbs made several radio calls to the higher-ups, trying to get authorization for us to go back out to the PZ, but it did no good. They kept ordering us to stay put. The thought of Becker and Schmidt still out there and possibly alive terrorized us. The commander told us that the weather had deteriorated to the point beyond operational minimums and Winfield's ship was returning to Kham Duc too. We knew better than to believe that. The real reason was that we had gotten the CCN men out, and that was all that mattered to them. They did not give a damn about Army personnel. I realized then that they considered us expendable.

Winfield had made it into the PZ. He extracted Anderson along with the rest of the special troops. That was it, the mission was deemed complete. We would not be allowed to return to try to get our two crew members out. CCN reasoned that since Becker and Schmidt did not make it back to the PZ, they must have been dead and that the weather was too bad to extract them. A nauseous feeling came over Dobbs and me. Deep down in our hearts, we knew that there was nothing that we could have done to change the situation, but it did not help. Dead or alive, Becker and Schmidt were still left out there. I realized these CCN troops, whom I had once thought so highly of, did not give a damn about us. We were laying our lives on the line and losing them to help them out, and that was the thanks we got. (We were put in for medals, Dobbs a Silver Star and myself a Distinguished Flying Cross, a medal that I was never to claim, left somewhere in the paperwork of the MACV-SOG.)

I was to find out years later that Anderson's mayday call went out over Guard frequency and was heard by some of our other ships back at Kham Duc. Capt. Michael Beaumont, who was Lt. Becker's platoon leader, was back at Kham Duc at the Petroleum, Oil, and Lubricants (POL), when the infantry commander came out to his ship and said that he was going to send out some troops for Beaumont to insert, to try to secure the area where Becker and Schmidt went down. A gun team was alerted and several Rattler and Minutemen aircraft arrived and refueled for the mission. Suddenly, they were ordered over the radio, "Not to return to the crash site and not to insert American troops." I was told that the infantry commander protested to our Division headquarters and was threatened with a court martial if he did not obey the order.[7]

No other personnel were listed as missing from this incident. The fate of the soldiers on the ladder remains unknown to this day. They were either recovered dead or alive at a later date, or more likely they were indigenous personnel and would not be listed on our casualty lists. Lt. Becker's family was told that he was shot down over Vietnam and was initially listed as MIA (missing in action). After a year, the classification was changed to killed in action body not returned (KIABNR). As of 2003 the crash site has been visited three times, but no remains of Lt. Becker or Spc4 Schmidt have ever been recovered.

Death was not new to me. My father passed away from cancer when I was eight years old, leaving my mother with five boys eleven to three years old, with me in the middle. I learned at an early age to be responsible for myself. But I was sick; sick of the war, sick of the army, just sick of everything. What a way to turn twenty! When I returned to my hootch that night, I had received some mail from back home. One of the letters was from my girlfriend, Carole. She wished me a happy birthday and then confessed that she had broken a promise to me. Before leaving for Vietnam, I had made her promise that she would not tell my mother anything that I wrote to her concerning action in the war. I did not want my mother to worry more than she already did.

When I had taken my cherry hits, I was so excited that I wrote home to my girlfriend, telling her all about the mission. I told her not to tell my mother, because I knew that every time my mom heard on the news about a chopper getting shot down she would imagine that it was me. When Carole got my letter, she got so upset that she called and told my mom about it, and now she was confessing this in her letter. It was the wrong day for me to be reading this letter. I was already upset about the mission, and now to receive this letter, I felt as if my life was spinning out of control. I was frustrated with what was happening in my life and that I had no control over anything. I needed to vent this frustration out on someone, and I wrongly took it out on her. I got so mad that I told myself that I would not write her anymore. I was going to deeply hurt someone that I really cared about. I received letters from her every day for weeks after August 15, but I did not return an answer until after Christmas.

The August 15 mission was pretty much the end of the special missions for the 71st AHC. They never did find any POW camps. We supported the troops at Kham Duc for two more weeks and then the ARVN started to pull out. In my opinion, the Kham Duc Campaign had been a failure. Charlie just pulled back and was content with making little contact, knowing that we would be pulling back from Kham Duc before the rainy season started.

The night before the final extraction, I was assigned to fly the flare ship out at Kham Duc. A flare ship was a helicopter loaded with flares that dropped them from high altitude. The flares would float down on their parachute, lighting up the dark skies for operations below. We would be spending the night parked alongside the airstrip. The ARVN had already pulled out all but five companies, so we were expecting an attack. The previous night, some sappers had crawled into the perimeter and turned some of the claymore mines around to face us rather than the attackers, which would injure our troops in the event the mines were set off. Luckily, our troops had discovered this the next morning. We were uncertain why Charlie had done this. Had they done this for psychological reasons, or were they planning an attack? Either reason made us anxious. Due to this claymore event, everyone at Kham Duc was prepared for some type of action that last night. We heard that the last time the Americans pulled out of Kham Duc, they ended up leaving two C-130 military transport planes behind in pieces. The C-130s got hit before they could get off the ground. We could still see the blown-up fuselages of these aircraft scattered alongside the runway. We did not want that to happen again.

After we loaded our aircraft with flares, we parked our Huey along the south side of the old dilapidated runway and set the cockpit up for a quick start in case of trouble. We were ready. If anything came up during the night, we could have our bird cranked and airborne within minutes. There would be several other lift birds spending the night with us. My AC was very short (a term we used when an individual was getting ready to go home), so he was quite nervous. As our crew sat around the aircraft eating C-rations for supper, the crew chief, gunner, and I talked about how Charlie was going to overrun us during the night. We could tell that our AC did not appreciate this talk, but it was fun to tease him. Heck, he was the one who was getting to leave this mess, not us.

It was one of those clear, late summer nights, with the sky extremely dark and moonless. We were sleeping with our bird, so I decided to crawl up and sleep on top of the roof of our helicopter. On the north end of the perimeter, there was a quad 50 machine gun, which was a trailer-mounted gun with four Browning .50 cal. barrels. Our troops would periodically open fire with the quad 50 and walk the perimeter of the airstrip, just in case Charlie was trying to sneak in. As the night went on, the air turned damp and chilly, and the suspense built. Little sleep was had by any of our troops. As the sun crept over the horizon, morning came, clean, clear, and fresh. No attack had occurred, just another night gone by. As the sun's rays lit the morning sky, we were released to return to base. We cranked up our bird and headed for home and a good day's sleep. Our company would finish the final extraction that day, with only light contact with Charlie. A Chinook helicopter went down, killing twenty-eight people. DT.639/QT.63B had been a worthless campaign.

CHAPTER 6

GOODBYE FRIEND

After the completion of the Kham Duc Campaign, we returned to flying in our old area of operations. We had several LZs located in our AO, with names like LZ West, LZ East, Mary Ann, and Hawk Hill. Hawk Hill was a fire-support base situated north of Chu Lai, a few clicks (kilometers) off Highway 1, halfway between Chu Lai and Da Nang. Because our AO was located directly west of Hawk Hill, we used the hill as our refueling point for the missions that we flew in our AO. An aircraft control tower managed the large volume of aircraft flying into Hawk Hill. In Nam, we always refueled hot, which meant that we kept the bird running while we refueled. Frequent refuelings and the quick turnaround times required to get back in the air necessitated this procedure. Rather than take the time to shut down the bird, we hovered up to the POL, set her down, then rolled the throttle back to idle. A Huey's fuel load was good for approximately two hours and twenty minutes of flight. With this short duration of flight, we would have to refuel several times during the day, so hot refueling saved considerable time. When we refueled hot, all personnel except one pilot would climb out and get clear of the aircraft in case it caught fire. The crew chief would first ground the aircraft with a wire to the ground, then ground the fuel nozzle to the aircraft, and finally start refueling. If the aircraft or the nozzle was not grounded properly, one spark could cause a fire or explosion; hence caution was always taken.

It was September 1970, and it had been four months since my arrival in Vietnam. The weather was changing rapidly as the monsoon season approached. The bright sun and clear skies suddenly were hidden from view by low-layered stratus clouds, and the hot temperatures had cooled. The rains had begun and would last for days. I had never seen so much rain in my whole life. We were still trying to fly resupply out in our AO, when the weather permitted; otherwise we did a lot of sitting. I found the down time from flying and the sitting around which accompanied it very boring and hard to handle. With nothing to keep our minds occupied, the time slowly dragged by. The hours seemed to turn into days. There was a lot of card playing and storytelling going on to help pass these dreadful days. You can imagine the homesickness and the daydreaming that took place.

September 14, 1970

Dear Larry,

Well, how are you? I'm feeling real good. My toe is still sore, but I can't do much about that. Today, I'm one third done with my tour. I sure still have a long ways to go. I just hope it goes fast. Tell mother that she can send me some uncooked popcorn and some Nut Goodies and sardines and some beef-jerky. I would really appreciate it.

Nothing really new has happened over here. You just get real bored. It's hard to remember what it was like back in the States, but the time keeps ticking away and pretty soon I'll be out of here. Well, I better close for now. Have fun at school.

One day toward the end of September I was sitting in our hootch, talking to Garrett, when Little Mac walked in. He told me that I needed to report to the Officers Club. There I found all the other ACs gathered, and they told me I had been chosen as an aircraft commander! They all congratulated and welcomed me aboard as an AC. I had been looking forward to this moment since I had arrived in Vietnam. I was no longer a newbie. I received my new call sign, "Rattler One-Seven," for me to be in charge of my own aircraft and have my own crew. This was the first time since I had arrived in Vietnam that I actually felt happy. To me, making AC was like graduating from high school. I would no longer have to change my flying technique for each AC that I flew with, trying to please him. I could finally be my own man. From that day on, I knew that I would have more control over what was happening to us out in the AO. No longer would I have to be a copilot and just sit there and only fly when given the chance by the AC. I had made it and I was truly happy for the moment.

During this same period someone in higher-higher, a term used for the people who gave the orders, thought it would be a good idea to send some of the pilots out to the field for aviation liaison. Our mission would be to educate the ground-pounders (i.e., infantry) about helicopters, especially the loading and unloading of the chopper and how the weight and location of the loads affected the weight and balance. I thought this was a very bad idea, especially after I became one of the few pilots selected for the duty. I could not picture myself sitting out at some fire-support base teaching people how to work with helicopters. I thought of myself as a pilot, not as an educator.

I had been flying my tail off during late September and early October. In Vietnam, we are only allowed to fly 140 hours in a thirty-day period. I had been busting my buns to get a couple of days off. The only way to get the days off was to exceed the 140-hour time limit within the thirty-day period. I was sitting there with more than 130 hours already with eight days left in my thirty-day period. I knew that I would be guaranteed a few days off, but then this aviation liaison mission came down and who was assigned? Me.

The sun was setting over the western ridge as I snatched my belongings and hopped off the Huey. Within seconds, the Huey lifted to a hover and departed, leaving me standing solo at the helicopter pad at LZ West. As I looked down from the fire-support base over the lush green countryside, I wondered what kind of life the peasants out there lived and why I was here. I went over and reported to the officer in charge, who in turn introduced me to the other officers stationed on the fire-support base. He took me over and showed me my living quarters for the next three days—a bunk in a small musty bunker shared with another lieutenant. I was not impressed.

It was already past 1800 hours, so I went over and had some chow. Afterwards I spent the rest of the twilight familiarizing myself with the fire-support base. Once it was dark, I went back to my bunker and read the *Stars and Stripes*. The *Stars and Stripes* was a government printed newspaper distributed to military personnel. The headlines read about a girl, back home, who had died. She was supposedly a famous rock singer and had overdosed on drugs, resulting in her death. I was not familiar with her at that time, due to my isolation from the real world after joining the army, but I was going to hear quite a bit of her music later. Her name was Janis Joplin. Music was one thing that I had not been able to keep up with while in the army.

I read the paper from cover to cover to help pass the time, and with nothing else to due, I hit the sack early. The next morning, I got up around 0600, shaved, and ate some breakfast. I was just finishing my breakfast when I heard that familiar "Whop, whop, whop," of the first helicopters coming in. I immediately went to work with the ground crews, helping them guide in the choppers and load them. I found it hard to watch our guys fly in with our birds, help load them up, and then watch them depart, leaving me stranded there. It was especially hard, since I had just made aircraft commander and I really wanted to be flying.

I spent the remainder of the day instructing and helping the ground personnel with the loading and off-loading of the choppers. Around 1600 hours of the first day, I decided that I had had enough—three days of this duty would definitely drive me bonkers. So I made arrangements with one of our ships flying in our AO to swing by and pick me up before returning home for the night. Without saying a word, I went and gathered my belongings and brought them up to the pad. When my ship dropped in to pick me up, I grabbed my belongings and jumped onboard. I thought to myself, "Goodbye, LZ-West." When I returned to the 71st company area that night, our company was so busy with the process of moving from our beach location over to the airstrip that no one noticed that I had skipped out.

The days were still slowly passing, and it was now the middle of October. The 71st was in the middle of a move. We would still be based at the Chu Lai airfield, but we were moving our company area from the beach to be closer to the east side of the airfield. The crews would no longer have to wait to take a truck to the flight line. We would now be close enough to walk over to the flight line from our company area, which would be a lot more convenient and would save us time starting in the morning and ending at night. We were taking over a company area that previously had belonged to the Marines. Their hootchs were much nicer than our old ones. Now we had a

8. Warrant Officer Pat Riley in the back with the author on the left and Warrant Officer Wendell Freeman on the right, standing behind a hootch in our company area at Chu Lai. (Photo courtesy of Terry Wasson.)

shower and a real toilet built into the hootch. Up to that point in our old company area, all we had were rocket tubes stuck in the sand for urinating, or what we called "piss tubes." For toilets, our men had taken 55-gallon drums, cut them in half, and positioned them under a wooden bench that had holes cut out for seats. What a marvelous toilet. Our enlisted men periodically had to pull these drums out from under the seat and burn the waste (one of the more unusual smells I noticed when I first arrived in the country). We were really excited about having a built-in commode and shower. At home, I had taken it for granted. The only downside was that our new quarters were a little tight, with eight to ten men assigned to a hootch previously lived in by four Marines.

It was one of those dreary, lazy, rainy days, and the wind was singing a high-pitched melody as she blew across the sheet metal-covered hootch. The rainy weather was getting me down. It was the first day of our move, and we had just finished cleaning out the last items from our hootch when the word came down—WO Peter Goodnight had been killed in action.

I was shocked. Goodnight was the first friend that I had known before going to Vietnam to get killed while I was in country. Peter's death was especially hard to understand and accept after I heard how he was killed. He had been out flying in his AO when he received a call to pick up a downed Huey crew. He and his crew responded immediately, locating the downed aircraft and hovering down into the LZ to pick up the crew. Confusion reigned over what happened next, but the word we received was that they first loaded a wounded soldier into the Huey, and then someone threw the wounded soldier's weapon into the aircraft. The weapon was an M60 machine gun, the same type of gun that we carried on our birds. It seemed that someone forgot to clear the weapon, and as it landed in the back of Pete's bird, it accidentally went off, hitting Pete in the head. They said he died instantly. What a senseless, useless way to die.

I had first met Peter Goodnight in flight school. We had been assigned to the same company and platoon during flight training because both our last names began with a G. Goodnight was from California. At first, I had not really liked him. Pete was pretty cocky, and because of this cockiness, everyone tended to take what he said the wrong way. But the better I got to know Pete, the more I started liking him, and before long we were friends. Pete and I spent ten months together during flight school, and upon graduation we were both assigned to Fort Carson, Colorado, for five months before shipping off to Vietnam.

One day while I was home on leave after flight school, but before reporting to Fort Carson, Pete and I were talking on the phone, and he told me that he had just bought a sports car. It was some type of

Volvo with which I was not familiar. I said I would be excited to see it. I pictured some fancy two-door sports coupe, because a lot of the pilots during and after flight school had bought Camaros, Corvettes, and Porsches. When I reported to Fort Carson, Goodnight came driving up in this boxy, four-door, blue Volvo. It was about ten years old. To Pete, it was a sports car; to me, it looked more like a family sedan. That was Pete.

Pete was always singing "Brown Eyed Girl." This must have been one of his favorite songs. While we were stationed at Fort Carson, we did not do a lot of flying, so we were assigned additional duties to keep us busy. Goodnight was put in charge of the PT department (physical training). During this time, the inspector general (IG) came through on inspection, and while checking our unit's records, he happened to notice that our aviation company had higher PT test scores than the cadets at West Point. Why? We actually had not been taking the PT tests; operations personnel instead had just been penciling in the scores, but instead of putting in realistic scores they were putting in extremely high ones. That was so typical for pilots; they always thought that they were the best. The IG suspected that something was not right, so he decided that part of our unit would be retested and our scores had better match our previous scores. Our company put Pete Goodnight in charge of this mess.

The next morning, Goodnight walked into operations and read off his list of the guys he had chosen to take the PT test, which involved such things as running a mile, doing sit-ups and push-ups, swinging from rung to rung on a ladder, and so forth. To my surprise, I was on the list. Here we were supposed to be friends, and he picked me. When I heard my name called, at first I was mad at Goodnight for choosing me for so much physical work, but later he explained why. He knew that he had to choose the guys who he believed could match the false high scores, and he remembered from our time in flight school that I was good at PT tests. In a way he was actually paying me a compliment by picking me, and being his friend, I now understood, although I still was not excited about having to take the PT test. (By the way, we matched the false scores.)

To me, Pete's death was a true tragedy. Pete had recently returned from being back in the States due to a death in his family, and now he was gone as well. It seemed like such a waste of a human life. From then on, every time I heard "Brown Eyed Girl," I thought of Pete. WO Peter Goodnight deserved better than what he got, and I miss him.

As we continued our move to our new company area, the monsoon season had arrived, and the weather was rapidly deteriorating. A typhoon was forecast to hit the South Vietnam Coast within the next few days, and we were already feeling the effects of it. The gusty winds warned us of the approaching storm. We had to get the helicopters secured and tied down before the storm hit the coast. Our flight line contained some old Marine revetments (walls built of steel and sandbags to protect aircraft from rockets and mortars), so our flight operations personnel decided that the best way to protect the Hueys from the storm would be to park them there.

The winds were blowing over forty knots as we cranked up our Hueys to reposition them into the revetments. It was a challenge to get the doors opened and closed without them blowing off in the high winds. As I sat in the cockpit cranking up the bird, I watched as the dirt and dust whipped around in front of us. I had never flown in such strong winds, and I knew that it was going to be tough to get the Hueys from our present position over in front of the revetments. Once we got the Huey on the ground in front of the revetments, the trick was to ground taxi them into the revetments.

To ground taxi a helicopter that does not have wheels is a skill in itself. When you add the strong winds and the close proximity of the revetments, it could be potentially disastrous. When ground taxiing a bird with skids, the pilot applies enough lift to get the weight of the bird off the skids, all the while still making sure that the skids are still in contact with the ground. The bird is light enough to move forward without being airborne. Once we had the bird light on the skids, we would ease the cyclic forward to move the bird. We carefully used our foot pedals to maintain directional control, to counteract the torque applied to the bird by this addition of power, plus the effect of the wind blowing against the side of the bird. With the wind blowing angular to the revetments, this was no easy feat.

I took a deep breath and slowly lifted the collective. Once the bird was clear of the ground, I turned her in the direction of the revetments. My bird was jerking from side to side and lurching forward as the gusty winds hit her. I felt like a pendulum swinging in a grandfather clock, as my bird swung beneath its rotor. I battled the wind with my controls as I rode her, like a cowboy riding a bucking bronco, over in front of the revetments and set her down. Now all I had to do was ground taxi her into the revetment. I refocused my attention to the job at hand and slowly and carefully ground taxied her into the revetment. One by one, our crews slowly got their Hueys into the revetments. Some of the flying was not very pretty, but we all succeeded in getting the choppers into the revetments without any damage. Once we had the birds safely inside, the ground crews went to work and strapped them down. With the typhoon just off shore and headed in our direction, we spent the whole night moving in the rain, hoping to get done before the brunt of the storm hit. What a mess. Everything and everyone got soaked.

9. Author's aircraft #405 in the maintenance hanger at Chu Lai. (Author's collection, photographer unknown.)

Our new area was about a four-block walk from the hootches to the flight line, a lot nicer than having to take the truck every time we went between the company area and the flight line. We now had a nice big hangar to house our maintenance facility and operations, and we had the two rows of Marine-style revetments for our choppers. One of the best things about our move was that our new mess hall was right across the road from our hootch. The move would be a good change for the 71st.

Our company was also starting to change. A lot of the old-timers, with their clique mentality and so-called esprit de corps, were leaving and going home, which meant that the new guys were no longer newbies. At the same time, a lot of new pilots were arriving, and most were commissioned rather than warrant officers.

As a new aircraft commander, I was starting to learn the ropes. When you were a copilot, you really did not worry a whole lot about the operations, because you were not given any responsibility. When you made AC, suddenly those responsibilities were all yours. To help the situation, Operations paired the new aircraft commanders with the experienced copilots for the first couple of weeks, to help them out. This was a good policy. Besides being responsible for your bird and crew, you now had to learn to fly the chopper from the left seat instead of the right. The first couple of days of flying from the left seat felt strange. Every time I shot an approach I found that my sight picture appeared lopsided, because the curvature of the nose bubble was in the opposite direction. Within a few days, I adjusted and discovered that the bird actually flew better from the left seat than the right. As a new AC I spent my first few weeks flying resupply missions out in our AO, with a few combat assaults thrown in.

Another responsibility that you acquired when making AC was that you were now in charge of when your crew fired their guns. This was a big responsibility, for if you were to give the wrong command, at the wrong time, it could mean life or death to the people on the ground. One day we were out flying, working with an infantry major. He was doing a high reconnaissance of his troops' area of operation, when he spotted some soldiers out in the open. Due to our altitude, we were unable to determine if they were friendly forces or Viet Cong. The major checked his map coordinates of these troops against his

10. Author on the left with Hubert Collins (right) standing in front of the O'club at Chu Lai. The entrance to the club has a pair of crossed rotor blades. (Author's collection, photographer unknown.)

location of where his men were operating and quickly decided that they were the enemy. He told me that he was positive that there were no "friendlies" in this area and ordered us to fire upon them.

If the major in charge of his troops did not know where his men were, who would? So I ordered our gunners to lock and load. I swung the chopper around and started a diving turn towards the ground where the enemy was located. I told my crew, "Go hot," and as my crew started firing, I dove the bird towards the troops. Suddenly, my gunner started yelling, "Stop firing, stop firing, they're friendlies!" I ordered my crew to stop firing, furious as I pulled the bird up from the gun run. I thought to myself, "Here this incompetent major ordered us to fire on his own men—thank God no one was hurt." It was lucky for the ground troops and me that I had a responsible gunner on board that day.

As an AC, my flying improved. I became more proficient at flying high overhead approaches and flying into confined areas. I worked hard to be one of our unit's best pilots. My confidence grew and it showed in my flying ability. I set a new goal—to become a senior aircraft commander. We called them "SACs" for short. The SACs were in charge of running the missions and the flights during the combat assaults. The SACs flew with and trained the new guys. Also, if the company was short of copilots for the day, they would schedule an AC with a SAC, and the SAC was in charge. To become a SAC, you had to be an AC for at least three to four months with no accidents or incidents caused by your flying skill, or lack thereof. If you met these requirements and the other SACs felt that you had the proper leadership qualities, you stood a chance of making SAC. The current SACs picked the new SACs when they needed to replace someone who was going home.

As an AC, my whole self-image changed. I could see that I was actually accomplishing something important. As a copilot, I always felt as if I was just a pilot's helper, not really a part of the crew. I remembered this feeling once I made AC, and so I tried to let my copilots accept as much responsibility as possible, teaching them as much as I could. Unlike when I first arrived in company, when no one would associate with the copilots except to harass them, I became quite good friends with the new pilots as well as with the old. During that time, we received several new pilots in our unit. Two of them in particular, Lt. Don Wolcott and Lt. Gene Britt, I took a liking to right away. They were both sharp and showed a sincere interest in becoming good pilots. I would spend a lot of hours flying with them.

CHAPTER 7

LAUGHING AND CRYING

The days seemed to run together as the months slowly passed by. I felt as if my whole life consisted of flying and sleeping. I did not think much about home anymore. The world I was living in was so different from the one in which I had been raised, to the extent that I found it extremely hard to emotionally relate one to the other. I was enjoying the flying and was really working at sharpening my flying skills, and I could tell that they were improving. How could they not? During an average day we were flying close to eight hours of actual flight time. I also found myself really getting "gung ho."

In war, situations occur that are life-threatening, yet when they are over, we laugh about them. I think this is a way of coming to terms with the reality of death and accepting that it had escaped us one more time. One of these situations happened to me one afternoon, in our company area. I had the day down (off) from flying, and with nothing exciting happening around our hootch, I decided to take a walk down to the Firebirds' hootch and see what was up. Firebird was the call sign for our gunships. We had eight UH-1C model Huey gunships in our company. A couple of my friends, WO Hubert Collins and WO Wendell Freeman, were gunship pilots, and they also had the day down. When I arrived at their hootch, Collins, Freeman, and a couple of the other pilots were hanging around with nothing to do, so we decided to play cards. We all grabbed our seats and started to play what we considered a serious game of Hearts. We had barely gotten the cards dealt when we heard a loud squealing sound overhead, followed by an earthshaking explosion, as a rocket came crashing down close to the hootch. The first rocket was immediately followed by a

11. Warrant Officer Firebird pilots (from left to right) Pat Riley, Mike Friel, Hugh Collins, Terry Wasson, and (seated in front) Wendell Freeman. (Photo courtesy of Wendell Freeman.)

second. Not being one to dally, I was out the door by the time the second rocket exploded, headed for the nearest bunker. As I cleared the doorway of the hootch, a third rocket exploded about a hundred yards from my position. I dove into the sand as debris flew everywhere. I quickly got up and scrambled over to a bunker located 150 yards from my prone position. Kicking up sand as I ran, I reached the bunker and dove in head first, landing on my belly. I had made it to safety, but no one else had.

As I sat there alone in the sandy bunker waiting for the rocket attack to end, I wondered what had happened to the other guys. I could not see the Firebird hootch from the bunker. Had I been the only one to make it alive to the safety of the bunker? Were the others dead? There was no glory in getting killed in a rocket attack. As I sat there alone in the bunker, a few more rockets came screaming in. Then as quickly as the rockets came, they stopped. After a few minutes of quiet, the all-clear signal was sounded. I quickly crawled out of the bunker and shook the sand from my Nomex flight suit. I ran back to the Firebird's hootch to find out what had happened to the guys. As I approached, I could see that the hootch was still standing but no dead bodies were lying in front. I pushed open the door to find all the guys standing there, laughing their heads off. Unbeknownst to me, the Firebirds had a built-in bunker under their hootch just for these occasions. While I was out risking my life dodging rockets, they merely had moved the card table to the side, lifted up the door to the bunker, and jumped in for security. I had to admit, it was funny.

One of the best laughs that I had in Vietnam was when my crew and I were headed for a night flare mission at Hawk Hill. It was approximately 1800 hours when we lifted off from the Snake Pit, the name we used to call the position on our flight line where we kept our Hueys. As we were the Rattlers, I thought the name was quite appropriate. We departed the Snake Pit and flew north towards Hawk Hill. Every night our battalion would station a flare ship at Hawk Hill, due to its close proximity to our AO, for any night flying that might be needed. It was one of those typical monsoon evenings. The skies were overcast, gray and cloudy, with light rain showers across the area. Due to the low ceilings, we decided to low-level up Highway One and drop in at Tam Ky first. Tam Ky had a MACV compound where we always could get a good dinner before reporting for our flare mission.

My copilot flew us up to Tam Ky. He shot an approach to the MACV compound helo pad and set the bird down. We secured the bird and headed towards the mess hall, which was run by the air force. We always tried to eat there as much as possible, because the air forces' food was considered great for Vietnam and definitely was better than what the army provided. As my crew and I walked down the path leading to the mess hall, I looked up and noticed a familiar face coming through the mess hall door. It was Jim Herron. Herron and I had gone to Cooper High School together back home in Minnesota. Seeing a familiar face so far away from home made me feel good. I called out to Jim and he stopped to chat. I told my crew to go ahead and eat and I would catch up with them later.

Herron was short, about five feet six inches tall, and stocky in stature. He also had a loud mouth. In high school, he was always cutting up and making fun of everyone, including me. We really were not good friends, but I did not dislike him, so it was still good to see him. Jim told me that he had been in Nam about four months and was a specialist in the air force. As we stood there talking, I suddenly realized that this was my chance to get back at Herron for all the people that he had made fun of back in high school. I asked Jim if he had had a chance to fly in a chopper yet, and when he said no, I said, "Well, let's go. I'll give you a ride."

We headed back down the gravel path leading to our bird, catching up on gossip as we walked. When we reached the bird, I told Jim, "Climb in the right pilot's seat and buckle up. I'll untie the blades and check over the aircraft. I'll be with you shortly." When I finished the walk around, I climbed in. As Jim finished buckling his seatbelt and shoulder harness, I told him, "Take the copilot's helmet and put it on so we can talk and hear each other." I then explained to Jim how to use the intercom. We sat there and talked about home as I cranked up the bird. By then the weather was misting. I lifted the bird to a hover and did a pedal turn into the wind. I nosed her over and off we flew.

If I could ever scare someone in the air, this would be my chance. I climbed the Huey up to about four hundred feet, which was just below the bases of the clouds. Then I quickly shoved the cyclic forward, which pointed the bird's nose down in a dive, diving towards the ground as we went. At the last second before ground impact, I pulled her nose up and headed towards a tree line. As we headed towards the tree line, I leveled the helicopter off with her skids twelve inches above the ground. Right when it looked as if we were going to crash into the trees, I popped the cyclic back and up we jumped, just missing the branches. Once we were clear of the trees, I dove back down over the deck, S-turning as we went.

I wanted this to be a ride that Herron would never forget. As we skimmed across the rice paddies, I checked out the expression on Herron's face. It was one of sheer terror. I knew that I had succeeded! I dedicated this ride to all the people back in high school that Herron had picked on and had made fun of. Who said revenge is not sweet?

One day, we had a new pilot assigned to our company. On his first day of flying out in our AO, he received the surprise of his life. He and his crew were supporting one of the local infantry units flying resupply to their troops. During one of their sorties out in the field, they set their Huey down in the LZ to drop off their load. As they were sitting there unloading their supplies, a gook in close to the perimeter of the LZ decided to take advantage of this fixed target. He opened fire and dumped a whole clip of ammunition right at the copilot. Thank goodness for the copilot, this gook was a bad shot. They returned fire and quickly exited the LZ. They flew back to a secure area where they set their bird down and checked out the damage. It was truly unbelievable what they found. On the helicopter, right behind the copilot's seat, they counted nineteen hits in the skin of the aircraft. How Charlie could have missed the copilot at that close range, we will never know. The AC said that as he counted the hits in the helicopter, the new pilot stood there and turned as white as a ghost. I do not believe the copilot was ever the same after that. What a way to get your cherry!

A strange thing happened after I had been in Nam a while. I found myself wishing that when I took hits to my bird, they would be closer to me than where they were. As long as no one was hurt, the closer the hits were to you, the better the war story. I had a close friend who had a great war story. While flying, he took a direct hit to his boot without even getting a scratch on him. Now that was a story to tell.

One day I was down sick with the flu. WO Bill Irby was flying in my place. He was down on the flight line doing his preflight, when a colonel came walking along and started yelling at him for not having a checklist in his hands while doing his walk around. Irby had this big handlebar mustache hanging underneath his nose, and as the colonel was yelling at him, Irby took his fingers and curled the ends of his mustache. This really pissed the colonel off, so the colonel walked over to the aircraft commander and started yelling at him. The colonel said, "Your copilot is gross!" The AC quickly replied, "No sir, he's not Gross. Gross is sick today!"

Along with the funny occurrences that happened were situations that made me feel like crying. But then there were situations that happened that I did not know if I should laugh or cry. One of these occurred while we were out flying a combat assault. Our company was doing an insertion into an area where some Viet Cong had recently been spotted. First, the Firebirds flew over and prepped the LZ using their miniguns and rocket launchers. We then went in hot with the Firebirds flying alongside, backing us up in a tight formation. Once we got down into the field, we quickly dropped off our infantry troops and departed.

As we were departing, I heard one of the Firebirds screaming over the radio that he had Charlie out in the open. Immediately, another Firebird radioed in screaming that Charlie was on the run, and they were rolling in on them. Then they all joined in. I had never heard such excitement before on the radio. This screaming continued for four to five minutes, as the gunships unleashed their intensive barrage of weapons. I knew that the Firebirds were blowing the hell out of Charlie. As we listened to the radio calls, the other pilot and I thought it was incredible to catch so many gooks out in the open. What luck! I could not wait to get back to the LZ to see the carnage. After we dropped off our troops, we had to fly clear of the area, so we were unable to see the battle taking place. When later we returned to pick up the infantry troops, I was ready to see the results of this massive assault. As our formation of birds shot their approach into the LZ, I was quickly scanning my eyes across the battlefield to see the hundreds of dead VC that the gunships had blown away. To my surprise, I counted only six dead VC. Were these boys getting carried away or what?

Another time we were flying resupply missions for an infantry unit, which had several platoons out in the field. I radioed the platoon and asked them to pop smoke. After identifying and confirming the color of the smoke, we executed a high overhead approach into their field location. We were sitting in the cockpit while the troops unloaded the supplies, when suddenly a sergeant ran over to my window, yelling "We've captured a VC. He's their head cook and bottle washer. I want you to take care of him for me." Then he gave me the thumbs up. Once the troops finished unloading the supplies, they tossed the VC into the back of our helicopter and we departed. As we climbed out of the LZ, I radioed a call to the headquarters of the unit that we were supporting. I informed them that I had their POW on board and that we would be bringing him back to their fire-support base. They responded to me, "Negative, you do not have a POW, there is no POW." At first this really surprised me, but then I realized what the sergeant meant when he said, "Take care of him for me." They wanted me to take this VC up to a couple thousand feet and throw him out. I know we had some pilots that would not think twice about doing it, but I was not one of them. We flew back to the fire-support base and dropped him off. If they wanted to kill him, they would have to do it themselves.

This POW story is even stranger than the last. We were out in our AO as usual, flying resupply. We swung down into the field and dropped off the supplies, and once again the ground soldiers loaded a POW on our aircraft. This enemy soldier had been hit several times and was severely wounded. Watching as the ground troops loaded him into our chopper, I noticed that his right arm was all but blown off. The only connection between his arm and his body was a tendon barely attached to his torso. As they loaded him on the Huey, they had to pick up his arm separately and set it on his stomach so that when they picked him up it would not drag alongside.

I had never seen anything like this before. I gave the controls to my copilot so I could study this man's wounds. I could not believe that he was still alive. He also had taken a direct hit to the head. This shot entered just behind his forehead, up and aft of his temple region. It blew a hole in his skull that was about one inch high and three inches across. I could look right into his skull and see his brain. I had never seen a human brain before, much less in a living person. Finally, as if the wounds to his arm and head were not bad enough, he had also taken a bad hit to the chest, what we called a sucking chest wound. As I watched him breathe, I could see his blood suck in and out of the wound in unison with his breath.

When we radioed headquarters to inform them that we had picked up a POW, to our surprise they told us to bring him in for questioning. That was the craziest thing I had ever heard. I radioed them back with a loud "Negative." I proceeded to tell them that he was too badly hurt for questioning and we were taking him over to the medivac pad. We flew directly to the closest hospital medivac pad and dropped him off. With all the damage to his body, I was impressed with the strength of this man's will to live. Later that evening, as we flew by the hospital on our way back to home base, I radioed the hospital to find out the status of this man. The doctor informed us that they had operated on the soldier immediately and had to amputate his arm, and amazingly he was still alive at that point. I do not know if this man ever lived or died, but I was truly amazed at his strength and determination to live and how much devastation the human body could withstand.

One of the pilots in our company, Conners, did one of the most disgusting things that I had ever heard of (his name has been changed to protect the guilty). Conners was a good old Southern boy from North Carolina. I got along with him fine and he seemed to be a pretty nice, normal guy, just your typical Joe Blow. He liked to brag about flying down Highway One after dark in his Huey with his lights off. The South Vietnamese rode up and down the highway on scooters and bicycles. He would take his Huey and fly low-level down the highway, waiting until he was quite close to the Vietnamese on their scooters and bikes. At the last second, he would flash on his landing light and watch as the Vietnamese would crash into the ditch, trying to avoid being hit by the helicopter. He thought this was funny.

One night, he was out doing his routine and waited a split second too long before he flashed on his landing light. It was too late—his helicopter skid ran right into the Vietnamese rider, throwing him from his scooter. You can imagine what was left of this person after being hit by a helicopter skid going eighty knots. Then to top it off, he was dumb enough to go back to the company area and tell the other pilots what happened, laughing as he told his escapade. Of course, nothing ever happened to him. The sentiment was that the person he just mangled or possibly killed was just a Vietnamese. No one cared. I was appalled at how our own people could treat other human beings so inhumane. It was not because they were the enemy, because these

South Vietnamese civilians were not. It was because they were of a different race. To many of our soldiers, the Vietnamese were not seen as humans because they were not Caucasian.

Periodically I would get a mission that would take me down to Duc Pho. Our sister company, the "Dolphins," were based there. Peter Goodnight had been with the Dolphins, along with my friends Buddy and Bob who I had met when I entered country. It was fun to get to see and talk with Buddy and Bob.

Duc Pho's main attraction was what everyone referred to as a "Steam and Cream." It was a Vietnamese sauna where a lot of the guys would go and get a good sauna, rub down, and whatever else that they could work out with the girls. I understood these girls made good money. Other than the sauna in the village, it was a typical military base situated on a high knoll a few miles in from the South China Sea. Occasionally, we would get to fly missions with our sister company in their area of operations. The Quang Ngai River was located in their AO. The river stretched westward from the China Sea a good distance into the countryside. Located on the south side of this river was a village called Quang Ngai. Alongside of the village, the American forces had built a compound with a stand that sold real hamburgers. This was unusual for Vietnam, so whenever we were flying in their area of operations, we always made an effort to drop in for lunch and have a hamburger and some french fries.

The aviation units in Vietnam had hootch maids, who were Vietnamese women and teenage girls from the local villages. The hootch maids were hired to come in during the day and do our laundry and polish our boots. We would pay them in Vietnamese money, and with the exchange rate being so good, their pay was equivalent to approximately five U.S. dollars a month. It was a cheap price to pay for someone to do your laundry and boots for a whole month. Down south, a lot of the pilots had live-in hootch maids. These were single girls who would move in with them for the year to provide the guys with sex and whatever other services they wanted. Some of these guys actually brought some of their hootch maids back to the United States as wives.

We were not allowed to have live-in hootch maids in our unit. We had one hootch maid for about every five guys. I personally enjoyed talking to the maids and gained a lot of insight into what the average

12. "A Vietnam Helicopter Pilot's Personal Assets." One of the many photos that the skull posed in. (Photo courtesy of Wendell Freeman.)

Vietnamese felt about the war and life in general. They told me that their main dream in life was to get married and raise a family. The South Vietnamese were a very family-oriented society. They were also a very poor people, and when you explained to them the way we lived back in the States, they had a hard time imagining it.

My hootch maid was a pretty lady. She was in her late twenties and was about five feet two inches tall, with a medium build and long black hair. She was married to an ARVN sergeant. One day, as I walked into our hootch, I noticed that she was sitting there eating what appeared to be French bread rolls. I asked her if she had baked them herself, and she asked me if I wanted to try some. I tried a roll, and it was really good. I did not care much for the mess hall food, so I asked if she would bring me a few rolls every day if I paid her, and she agreed. I told her to just leave the bread rolled up in my bunk. This worked out great, especially on the nights when I got back late and was tired. I did not have to worry about walking down to the mess hall to get something to eat. I would eat my rolls and then just go to bed. Occasionally I would come across a bug or two in the bread. When that happened, I would just tear the bug out and continue to eat the rest of the roll.

It was always fun to tease the hootch maids. We found out that they were quite superstitious. During one of the many rocket attacks, WO Mark Dobbs and WO Roger Theberge, seeking cover from the explosions, dove into an old bunker. Once inside the bunker, they found a human skull. The skull had a couple of bullet holes in it; otherwise it was in excellent condition. They grabbed it and brought it back to our hootch. One morning when I had the day down, I took the skull, set it on my pillow, and put my arm around it as if I were hugging it. I pretended that I was asleep. The hootch maids came walking into our hootch and took one look at me with my arm around the skull and started screaming their heads off. We thought it was funny.

A lot of the guys took the skull and posed for pictures with it. Sometimes they would put a flight helmet on it. Other times they would take a uniform and fill it up with sand, lay a machine gun or rifle across the body, and then put the skull on the body's neck with a combat helmet strapped to the skull. It made for a great picture. I was in the first platoon and our patch was the Widow Makers. We had a skull-and-crossbones logo on a black spade for our patch, so I kind of looked at the skull as our mascot.

13. The patch worn by the first platoon. The hat really sets off the skull and crossbones and gives the patch a gruesome look. (Author's collection.)

CHAPTER 8

THE HOLIDAYS

November 22, 1970

Dear Mother,

I have today off because I have to fly tonight. I'm in good health. They sent the Americal Division home so they just changed us to the 23rd Infantry Div. All it was was a name change. My platoon leader from Fort Carson, who was stationed here, got killed last week. Quite a few people from Carson have been getting it. I am enclosing a money order for Christmas. Please go ahead and buy the kids and yourself presents from me. If there's any left, go ahead and buy the Christmas tree with it. Please spend it all. I hope this letter gets to you in time. The mail is starting to slow down quite a bit. I'm still trying to keep my morale up. It's pretty hard sometimes. Well, I better run now.

Holidays were some of the longest and loneliest days of my Vietnam tour. Those days were spent thinking about home and wondering what my family and friends were doing. I wondered how they all were and if they were missing me as much as I was missing them. I usually tried not to think about home because it made me feel lonelier and depressed. I discovered that the less I dwelled on it, the better off I was. But when the holidays came around, I could not help but think about home.

Fourth of July in 1970 was the first major holiday that I spent in Vietnam. It came and went without mention of its passing. This was the first Fourth of July that I had ever spent away from home. The previous year, my class had received a leave during our break in flight school, and I was fortunate enough to make it home for the holiday. My family's tradition was to celebrate the Fourth by having a picnic in the late afternoon, after which we would all climb into the car and go see the fireworks. This was the custom of many of the families back home. But in Vietnam there would be no picnic or fireworks for me this Fourth, just a mental note of the days passing.

Thanksgiving came, and I was scheduled to fly. I was hoping I would have the day off. That morning, like every other morning, I got up at 0430 hours and headed down to the flight line. I always skipped breakfast for a little more sleep and a stronger stomach. I found it hard to get into a helicopter with a stomach full of the Army's mess at that time of the morning. We walked down to the flight line, completed our morning preflight of the aircraft, cranked up our bird, and flew to the first unit that we were assigned to support for the day. The sun was breaking over the horizon as we turned on our final approach to Hawk Hill.

Hawk Hill was a combination fire-support base and troop headquarters for several of the ground units that we flew support for in our AO. After parking the bird and shutting her down, we got out and secured her blades. The copilot and I then walked over to the unit's headquarters that we would be supporting for the day. When reporting in, we heard that our mission would be to fly turkey out to the troops in the field. I thought this was a cool mission, being that it was Thanksgiving. Along with the turkey we also would be flying a priest, whose call sign was Sky Pilot, to give a blessing to the troops. The officer in charge briefed us on the location of the different units and how we should accomplish this mission. He then told us that the turkey would not be ready until 1000 hours. I looked at my watch, and it was only 0700 hours. With three hours to kill, we immediately headed to the mess hall for some breakfast. It was a few minutes before ten when a specialist came over to our chopper and notified us that the turkey was ready. It was time for us to do our thing.

The cooks loaded the hot turkey dinners into mer-mac cans (insulated green canisters) to keep the food warm until we could deliver it to the troops. Our crew loaded the aircraft with enough chow to feed four to five platoons. The Sky Pilot climbed in as they finished loading the bird. We cranked up our bird and departed from Hawk Hill, heading west toward our area of operations. We had been given the basic grid coordinates of each unit at the morning briefing, so I already had located the first unit's position on our map and flew as close to that location as possible. Once we were in their vicinity, our second step was to raise radio contact with that unit on the ground. "Bravo One, Rattler One Seven, over." "Roger Rattler One Seven, go ahead." "Bravo One, we're inbound with chow and Sky Pilot, pop smoke, over." "Rattler One Seven, smoke's out." I looked down and could see a red smoke blowing in the field below. "Roger Buddy, we have red smoke, over." "Rattler One Seven, we confirm the red smoke, over." "Roger Bravo One, we're headed in."

Once we identified Bravo One's red smoke and got the proper confirmation, we determined the wind direction and set up for a high overhead approach. Before the dust had settled, the troops were at the bird's skids unloading the mer-mac cans, as the priest jumped out. Within seconds we were pulling pitch, and our bird lifted off climbing for that safe haven called altitude. We then banked our chopper towards the new heading that would take us to the next ground unit.

We shot approaches to a couple more of the ground units, executing the same high overhead approach with a quick in-and-out maneuver. By the time we completed these two drop-offs, the troops at Bravo One had finished their dinner, and it was time for us to return to pick up the priest and the empty cans. Once we had the priest on board, we were off to the next unit. We would not be able to get the Sky Pilot to all the ground units because of lack of time and security on the ground, but we did get them turkey, and they sure seemed to appreciate it. That was the way I spent Thanksgiving in Vietnam. I was a little upset when I was first told that I would have to fly on Thanksgiving, but bringing a bit of the holiday cheer to those troops in the field, and seeing their appreciation, made it truly worthwhile. Helping our troops to have a real turkey dinner on Thanksgiving made a memorable Thanksgiving for me.

One of the reasons that I liked being a warrant officer more than a commissioned officer was that we received the respect of being an officer without the additional duties associated with a commission. At least that was the way it was supposed to work in the army. A warrant officer was trained to be an expert in his field (mine being a helicopter pilot) and to perform the associated duties. I was soon to find out that it did not always work out that way. Why I received this next assignment, I'm still not sure. I figured that somewhere along the line I must have stepped on someone's toes, and they wanted to return the favor.

The Christmas season was at hand, and we were all trying to get into the spirit of the season as best we could, considering our surroundings. My mom had sent me a miniature Christmas tree with a care package of goodies. Most of the other guys in our hootch had also received care packages, so we had a good taste of a home-fashioned Christmas without the home. My girlfriend's parents sent me a little tree and a holiday gift package that contained a canned ham, salami, and an assortment of cheese, so we had a lot of goodies that were associated with the Christmas holidays.

I had been wondering how a group of grown men would react to spending Christmas without their families. This would be the first Christmas away from home for most of us. I also realized that it had to be the hardest on the married fellows with young kids back home, but they did not seem to show it. As Christmas approached, everyone appeared to get into the holiday spirit. I think we all had a little kid left inside of us when it came to Christmas. A few days before the holiday, I was given orders to report to the battalion commander's office at 1900 hours sharp, which meant that I had been picked for some kind of special detail. I thought to myself, "What a lucky guy."

The meeting at battalion headquarters was short and to the point. All of us at the meeting had been chosen to be officer of the guard for our respective company on Christmas Eve. Officer of the guard was normally pulled by a commissioned officer, but for some unexplained reason, I was chosen instead. The colonel went on to explain that last Christmas Eve some troops decided to celebrate by shooting up the perimeter, and it got out of control. Several of the other guards on duty joined in the shooting, and by the time they finally got the shooting stopped, one of our men had been shot and killed. Our colonel was going to make sure this never happened again, and that was why we were there—we would be the ones to prevent it. Normally the officer of the day (OD) stayed at headquarters, and then at certain times of the night, he or the sergeant of the guard went out and checked the guards along the perimeter, but that was not to be for us. Instead, the colonel decided that the officers would stay right with the guards, in the bunkers, on the perimeter. This way, if any of the guards started firing in celebration, we would be there and would be held responsible for not stopping it. The only trouble I could see with the colonel's plan was that there were more bunkers for me to cover than there were me! I could only be in one bunker at a time, yet I was responsible for several bunkers along the perimeter.

I had been planning on flying Christmas, and after having such an enjoyable Thanksgiving flying, I was hoping to repeat the experience—and now this. I was steaming as I walked back to my hootch thinking about spending Christmas Eve on guard duty in a bunker. I was not an infantry officer. If I had wanted to spend time in a bunker, I would have joined the infantry. What really bothered me was that over half of our pilots were commissioned officers, and duty officer was their duty, not a warrant's. I wondered why I had been picked. I had already put in my request to fly on Christmas Day, but I knew that there would be no changing it. In the army, your orders were it. There was no appeal allowed to anyone who had the authority to change them. The army called this the chain of command.

On Christmas Eve, I slept in and got up around 1000 hours. It was a warm humid day, not like the crisp, cold Christmases back home. Being from the midwest, we always seemed to have a white Christmas, but it would not be a white one for me this year. As I pulled myself out of my sleeping bag, I noticed that the air felt heavy. It hung deep in my lungs like a dense fog. I thought to myself, "At least I won't have to run around and do any last minute Christmas shopping." I wrote to my mom at the beginning of December, due to the time it took for our mail to get home, and wished my family a Merry Christmas. I asked my mom to send my girl a dozen roses for Christmas. That was the extent of my Christmas shopping.

My mom wrote back and said that my aunt from Minneapolis had asked her what she could do for me, since I was over in Vietnam. My mom told her that she could send me a box of Christmas cookies. It was really hard to explain to someone back home how much a box of anything from the States could cheer you up. It was a link from home, a reminder that you had not been forgotten, that you actually mattered to someone. My aunt sent me a Christmas card with a note saying, "We would have sent a box of homemade cookies, but they would have gotten smashed in shipping so we didn't bother." This note really was a downer, and it made me feel depressed. It was not the lack of cookies, but the thought that she did not seem to care enough to chance it. When you were away from home in a combat zone, it was important to know that there were people who cared enough about you to send a package to lift your spirits. Heck, we would have eaten the crumbs! We all needed a boost once in a while, and especially during the holidays.

Roger Theberge, Mike Carlisle, and a few of the guys had the day down, so we sat around swapping stories while we shared the Christmas treats from home. I was supposed to report to the orderly room at 1630 hours for OD, so I walked down to the mess hall early and got a quick bite to eat. It was around 1600 hours when I finished eating and returned to our hootch to get dressed. I would not be allowed to wear my Nomex flight suit for OD, so I dug into my locker and pulled out a set of jungle fatigues. I never wore fatigues, just flight suits, so my fatigues looked so new that everyone would think that I had just arrived in country. I felt like a newbie all over again. I slapped together my pistol belt, grabbed my steel helmet, and headed down to the orderly room. There was no holiday cheer on this old boy's face.

When I reached the orderly room, I met with the sergeant of the guard, and we went over his duties for the night. By the time I finished his briefing, it was time to have the troops fall in for their inspection. The purpose of this inspection was to check the troops for proper dress, and to make sure that their weapons were clean. I had not done an inspection like this since flight school. I walked over to the sergeant of the guard, who was standing in front of the troops and nodded to him. He turned and faced the troops, then yelled, "Platoon, atten hut." The troops snapped to attention. The sergeant then turned to me and said, "Sir, all present and accounted for." I yelled, "Prepare troops for inspection." The sergeant did an about face and yelled, "Platoon, dress right dress." The troops were now ready for my inspection. I personally was not a lover of the military and felt almost like a hypocrite doing such an inspection, but I knew better than to show it. I thought to myself, "Chuck, just play the game." So I acted the part. As I walked down the line of soldiers, I carefully looked over each soldier's appearance and checked a few weapons. The troops looked good, so I gave them their orders for the night. I wanted to make sure that they understood that there would be absolutely no shooting unless the enemy was spotted. I did not want to have a repeat of last year.

Once I was done giving my orders to the troops, the sergeant called out his order, and the troops quickly filed into the trucks that were standing by, ready to take us to the perimeter. When the last of the troops were loaded, I climbed into the duce-and-a-half truck (a two and one-half ton troop carrier) and we headed down the bumpy, sandy trail leading toward the eastern perimeter. Sitting there in the back of the truck with the troops as we rode toward the perimeter, I could feel that it was not a very friendly atmosphere. No one wanted to be there and it showed. Everyone just stared down or at each other.

The perimeter that we were assigned to guard was set up with watchtowers. These towers were spaced approximately every hundred yards along the perimeter. Between each of these watchtowers, barbed wire and concertina wire stretched along the perimeter, with claymore mines placed in the wire. Three men were assigned to each tower, and they were to rotate watches. I stationed myself in the center tower. This tower had a landline connected to the other towers so I could communicate between all the towers. For some unknown reason, the landline was inoperative. The towers consisted of a square room, about ten by ten feet, elevated approximately twenty feet off the ground with a ladder running up to the room. As I pulled myself up into the tower, I saw that it had a couple of cots, some ammunition, and the controls for the claymore mines.

I was expecting a quiet night because the North Vietnamese and the South Vietnamese governments had announced their usual Christmas truce and cease-fire. The only job that the guards really had to do while on duty was to watch the perimeter to make sure the truce was being honored. We had been taught in basic training how to continually scan back and forth along the perimeter to detect any movement. Darkness arrived around 1800 hours. Rather than assign the watches to the other two guards, I decided that we would draw lots in our bunker to see who would man each watch. I drew the second watch.

While you were on guard duty, you were supposed to hold the noise level down to a minimum so you could listen for any movement or sound coming from the perimeter that might indicate a sapper. This quietness created a very peaceful feeling.

As the duty officer, I was required to periodically check each guard post to make sure that everything was ok and that the guards were not smoking pot or doing dope, which was quite common. I decided to let the sergeant of the guard make the rounds instead of me, so I would not have to leave my outpost on the perimeter. Around 2300 hours, I received a call on the radio from one of the towers to the south of my location. The soldier on the radio reported to me, "One of my guards is going crazy. A big bug has flown into his ear, and he can't get it out. He's sticking a needlenose pliers into his ear trying to remove the bug." I told the soldier to stop him from sticking the pliers in his ear—it could puncture his eardrum—and I would be right over. I grabbed my M16 and climbed down the ladder. I headed down the perimeter toward the tower where the soldier was having the problem. As I worked my way down the perimeter, I realized that this was not the place to be taking a casual stroll. Truce or no truce, there was still a good chance that Charlie might shoot me, and there probably was a greater chance of being shot by my own men. I proceeded with caution as I worked my way down the perimeter with those wonderful thoughts running through my mind. Suddenly, I noticed a jeep headed in my direction. It pulled up to me and in it was my sergeant of the guard. He motioned for me to hop in. When we arrived at the guard tower, sure enough, there was this big black man digging around in his ear with pliers. He was yelling that the loud buzzing was driving him crazy. By the way he was acting, I believed him. I immediately pulled him off the perimeter and sent him to medical. We then had to get a replacement.

By the time I returned to my post, the first shift had ended and mine was just starting. One of the guards in my watchtower had a small transistor radio with him. That was definitely against regulations, but since it was Christmas Eve, I turned it on at a very low volume and tuned it to the Armed Forces Radio Station broadcasting out of Da Nang. To my delight, they were playing Christmas songs. I sat there during my watch listening to Christmas carols, while constantly scanning the perimeter for Charlie, thinking about past Christmases. Periodically, off in the distance, I saw a firefight between Charlie and some ARVN troops. As I watched, the shooting would flare up, then die down, then flare up again. I thought to myself, "Can't they even keep a Christmas truce?"

It was one of those long, dark, lonely nights. I wondered what my family was doing. Were they celebrating Christmas like the other years, just without me? Were they missing me as much as I was missing them? Then there was my girl. Even though I had not written her but once since August, I wondered if she was having a nice Christmas. I thought about the previous year when we had had such a good Christmas together. Did she miss me? I thought about my friends and all the Christmases past. I had never really enjoyed family get-togethers with the relatives when I was home, but now I was missing them. For once in my life, I was seeing Christmas in a different light. I realized that it was the people who made Christmas, not the gifts and fancy food, but being with your loved ones. Christmas was a time for togetherness.

When it came time for the third watch to start, I told the guard that was scheduled for it to go back to sleep. I would finish his watch for him. I did not feel much like sleeping. It was a hard night, but in a strange way, it was one of my best Christmases. On that lonely night, I learned a lot about myself and about the true spirit of Christmas.

The night ended without any disturbances, so we gathered up our equipment and I headed back to our hootch for some sleep. Since I had been up all night, I spent Christmas day sleeping. The guys said they had a special Christmas dinner over at the mess hall, but it was over by the time I woke up. Other than that, it was just another typical day in Vietnam.

The day after Christmas I was back flying. One of our first sorties was to transport a band that had been playing up at Da Nang for Christmas. We were to pick up the group and fly them down to Chu Lai. Periodically, the higher-ups would bring in bands to entertain the troops to help boost their morale. They would put on what was called a "floor show." The members of most of these bands were Oriental, mostly Korean, and they would play rock-and-roll music. They always had sexy girls who go-go danced along with the music.

We flew up to Da Nang where we had been ordered to pick up the band. As the band members walked toward our bird, I could tell by their high cheekbones that they were all Koreans. All the soldiers were gawking at the female members, and I could not blame them. As they climbed into our aircraft, one of the girls came over and sat down on the pedestal that was situated between our pilots' seats. Normally that area was off-limits, but I quickly realized that this was a special occasion. Since we rarely got to fly women, I decided that it would be all right. I had already been in country for seven months, and the scent of a woman had been absent from my senses since I had arrived. As I began to crank up the bird, my senses picked up the sweet scent of this gorgeous women, sitting right next to me with her lovely smelling perfume. For a short moment, I was transferred out of my olive drab, cold-blooded metal machine into a flower-scented heavenly plain. I was totally amazed at how a sweet scent of perfume on a woman could smell so good and make me feel so fine. As we flew back to Chu Lai, I sat back and enjoyed the moment, because I knew that it would be fleeting. That trip was one of the most enjoyable flights of my tour. I would remember that scent for years.

Talking about floors shows, Bob Hope had been performing in Da Nang the week before Christmas with his United Service Organizations (USO) show. It was the typical military crap. They allowed just a few chosen men from each company to attend his show. We all knew who was chosen. It was not the soldier out in the field who had been fighting the war and really deserved to go. It was the higher-ups along with some of the guys who worked at headquarters, none of whom had fired a gun since advanced infantry training (AIT).

A lot of people believe that if you went to Vietnam you were automatically out in the field fighting the Viet Cong. This was not so. I would estimate that about one in ten Vietnam vets ever saw real combat. For every soldier who was fighting out in the field, you had approximately nine guys back in the security of their company area supporting him. You had all the guys in administration, in supply, and in the motor pool, all of whom never left the safety of the compound. I felt that they should have chosen the guys who were out in the field and doing the actual fighting to see Bob Hope, not the headquarters guys. I wondered if our CO enjoyed the show.

14. Author's bird sitting on one of the pads at the MACV compound at Tam Ky. (Photo courtesy of Pat Callahan.)

As I had mentioned earlier, we liked to fly into Tam Ky because of the great food that was always served at their mess hall. Because the Tam Ky compound was located in the middle of the village of Tam Ky, the helicopter pad was fenced in with chain-link fencing and concertina wire strung along the top, to keep the civilians from coming over to the helicopters and possibly fragging one or stealing our equipment.

Every time I landed at the Tam Ky helicopter pad I always saw a lot of little kids hanging around on the other side of the fence. They would stop playing and watch as we took off and landed. Several times when I had a little time on my hands, I would go over and talk to the kids. I really enjoyed messing around with them. As the months passed, I began to know some of the kids. It was a couple of days after Christmas, and I still had the canned ham that my girlfriend's parents had sent me. I also had a lot of hard candy left over, so I decided to take this ham and candy up to Tam Ky and give it to my little friends.

We set the helicopter down on the landing pad and shut her down. I took the canned ham and candy and walked over to the fence where the kids were playing. There was a double fence with about six feet of spacing between the two of them, so anything that I would give to the kids I was going to have to throw across this space. There was a really cute little girl whom I had seen several times before. She was about eleven or twelve years old. I motioned for her to come over, but she was very shy and timid, and I could not get her to come right up to the fence. So I took this canned ham and tossed it over to her, and she ran right over and picked it up. Well, this really got the attention of the other little kids, and they all ran over to the fence.

My crew also had brought some treats for the kids. So we started tossing treats over to the four or five kids that were there. To our surprise, out of nowhere numerous kids suddenly appeared on the other side of the fence. They were all yelling and screaming for candy. We had no idea where they all came from, but we had definitely created a scene. We looked at each other and decided that we had better get out of there as quickly as possible. The four of us threw what candy we had left over the fence then sprinted back over to our chopper, jumped in, and cranked her up as fast as we could. I could see that the kids were still screaming for more as I lifted our bird to a hover. We departed Tam Ky, leaving the commotion and the kids behind. It had seemed like such a good idea at the time! Even though we had caused a stir, I was glad that we had done it.

New Years came and went without anything significant happening. It was hard to believe it was even a new year. It just seemed like another typical day to me. Around the first of the year, I was assigned a new gunner named Pat Callahan. Pat was originally from Dallastown, Pennsylvania. He had been a "crunchy" (a contraction of "gravel cruncher," meaning infantry soldier) down south and had contracted malaria while he was out in the field. Pat had been in the hospital with malaria, and when he got better, he was assigned to the 71st.

One of the guys in our unit had a portable tape recorder and was always exchanging tapes with his wife back home. I thought that this was a great idea, so I decided to send a tape to my mom. I borrowed this guy's recorder and make a tape. (What follows is the exact tape as I made it. The only editing that was done was to take out personal talk that I felt would be of no interest to the reader and had no bearing on my tour.)

> *Hello, a late Merry Christmas. I decided that I'm going to try to send a tape. I don't know how it will turn out, but I figured trying is better than nothing! Today's January 3rd. I'm down today because we are allowed one hundred and forty hours a month flying and I have over one hundred and forty hours. So I guess that they decided that I deserve a day down. It's kind of bad weather now; it's quite a bit of rain, about the coldest that I've seen it yet.*
>
> *I hope you all had a real nice Christmas and a pretty good New Years. It's kind of hard to believe that it's 1971 already. I'm glad it is, 'cause four more months and I guess I'll be leaving here. I had a pretty enjoyable Christmas myself for being over here. Christmas Eve I spent the whole night, out in a bunker, on bunker guard. So that kind of stunk, but I guess that made a pretty good Vietnamese Christmas. It really could have been a lot worse off. I was pretty happy about it. I've been flying a lot, pretty tired, but good morale. I haven't been homesick hardly at all. I guess it's because I'm pretty used to being away. I'll be glad to leave here. I want to thank you for all the Christmas gifts. It really helped Christmas around here. I really appreciate it. I know that I haven't been writing as I should, but it is really hard to find the time to write a lot. I hope that you understand that.*
>
> *I guess it's in the middle of winter back home now. We're in the monsoons. It seems like the monsoons are going to never end. Actually, I hope that they stay for quite awhile because I would rather have it be cold like this than I would hot and dry. My flying has been coming along real good. I got quite a few hours now and I've been pretty tired, but I'm getting good food and a place to take a shower every night. So it's really not too bad.*

I've been hearing quite a bit from Steve Djerf. He seems to write me about once a week. It's kind of nice to hear from him. Haven't heard too much from anyone else.

It's kind of different talking into a mike with no one to talk back. All I do is talk and see what comes up.

Jim, I guess you're still waiting to go to basic training. Well, I wouldn't worry too much about it. It seems that they have passed so many rules nowadays that people in basic training can't even harass the trainees any more. I don't know if it is for the good or bad. I never liked basic, but I guess the training, when you think about it, is kind of good for you. It kind of shows you and gives you more will power, I guess.

Well, I guess I'm kind of glad that I came over here, especially knowing that I'll be going home in about four months. I've learned a lot. I guess this has helped me to find out more what life is really about, rather than think what life is about as so many of the younger kids do. 'Cause I guess over here, you find out that life is a lot different than what you read in the books. Even though I dislike it so much, I'll really be glad when I get home, that I came over here and it's helping my flying out.

When I leave here, I'll have a total of 1500 hours of flying and hope that I'll be able to line up a job. I really dig flying and I just hope that I can find a good job. I realize more that I'll have to go back to school for a couple of years and get a better education. 'Cause I guess the way the world is set up now days that you don't get any where without it.

It's really hard to think back, to remember what it was like, before I came over here and it seems like I've been here for a lifetime. I guess it's because so much has happened everyday. So much and so many things happen to you that it seems like a life span and it's really hard to remember what it was like right before I came over here. I guess it will take a while to readjust back to the world. I don't think I'll know how to talk to a girl. It'll be kind of weird.

It will take a while to relax. It will be really hard to relax, but I guess in a couple of weeks I'll be able to relax. 'Cause right now you can tell and measure in everyone, the longer they stay here, they're a lot more nervous. Things bother them a lot more. Living together, we're kind of cramped in space. It makes it kind of hard. I don't think that I'll be taking an R&R, 'cause really, I don't know who I would take it with. I think I'll just save the money and maybe buy me a motorcycle when I get home.

I really enjoy getting the Sunday paper. It makes me realize that there's still the world back there. I read the Sunday paper and the way that they talk about the war; I think that everybody's forgotten that there is a war in Vietnam, back there. It's kind of funny to see what I read in the newspapers and then see how it really is! In a way, it's kind of sad, but I guess they just know what's going on by what the reporters say. I guess that's what makes a newspaper.

I really enjoy getting the letters even though I don't write back all the time. 'Cause on the average day, we get up at either four thirty or five o'clock and make it down to the flight line by five thirty. You got to pull a preflight of your bird and our off time is normally six o'clock. Anyways, we don't get back till eight or eight thirty and you're so tired that you want to get something to eat and mainly relax. Most of the time, I try to get to bed, but we have an open bay type building here and it's about the size of our bedroom upstairs. We have six people crammed into it so we just don't get too much sleep. Any sleep that you can get you just kind of scrounge up.

I'm up for SAC, that's senior aircraft commander. That's about the highest that you can go. It's just really a complimentary gift, I would say, given to the top aircraft commanders who have so many hours and have flown so many months in Vietnam without having any accidents or incidents. I haven't had any accidents yet. I've been pretty lucky, I guess. I try to think I'm a pretty good pilot, so I hope I get it.

I'm really looking forward to leaving here. Time goes by quick, yet each day goes by so slow. I hope my car is O.K. I try not to think too much about home. It just makes things a little rougher, more depressing.

Now, I'm just looking forward to Easter, 'cause the only way that you can really relate time around here is by the holidays. You don't have weekends and the time just goes and goes and goes, but when you hit a holiday you can kind of relate to it and say look, I'm this far done already. Now, all I got to do is say I've got eight months behind me and four to go.

I hate to admit it, but my hair is starting to recede a little bit. My hair got real thin for a while. I imagine it's from the climate and wearing my helmet a lot, cutting down the circulation to my hair. I hope it will grow back when I get back to the world. I think I'm really in pretty good shape I don't think I look too bad at all. I really don't feel real bad.

I guess that will be all for now. Mother, I want to thank you again for writing as much as you do and sending the Christmas gifts. I really appreciate it. Well, before you know it, I will be coming home and I hope it seems like before you know it any ways. I guess that's all for now.

That would be the only tape that I would send home.

We had a warrant officer who worked in maintenance whom I liked, named Paul Flannery. He was one of the few warrant officers that I had met who did not have his wings. Paul sure had a story to tell. Paul had gone through WORWAC just like the rest of us. During the final weeks of flight school every student was given a final flight physical, and when Paul took his, he flunked the depth perception test. Why had this not been discovered on his initial flight physical? Paul had already completed most of his flight training without any problems. After more than eight months of flight school, they told him that he was unable to fly. Then to make matters worse, instead of flunking him out of flight school, they made him graduate and then permanently grounded him. If they had washed him out of flight school, as they should have, he would only have had eleven months of obligation left to the army. By forcing him to graduate and get his warrant, he was automatically signed up for three more years. Of course, with those three more years came his tour in Vietnam.

Talk about a screw job! Right after they forced him to graduate from flight school, they sent him to Aircraft Maintenance Officers

Course (AMOC) to learn maintenance on the choppers. Upon completion of AMOC, he received orders to go to Vietnam. As Paul sat there telling me this story, I decided that I would have to get him some well-deserved stick time out in our AO. One afternoon Paul had a few hours off, so I arranged for us to return to the company flight line and pick him up. I tried to get my copilot to take the rest of the day off, but he was a lieutenant and was afraid that if we got caught he would get into trouble. Being the aircraft commander, I ordered the lieutenant to go back in the gunner's spot and had the gunner get lost for a couple of hours. I then put Flannery in the copilot's seat and let him fly, giving him a couple hours of flying in our AO instead of just going on maintenance hops.

In mid-January, I was lying around my hootch one afternoon, having the day down from flying, when Mark Dobbs came in and grabbed me. The SACs had just had a meeting to pick the new SACs, and they had chosen me. I was really excited and pleased. This was a great honor—only the best pilots were chosen to be SACs, the leaders. I had my doubts if I would ever make SAC, being a non-drinker among a tight fraternity of drinking buddies that the SACs were. I was not sure if they would pick me. But they did. Now I knew that they recognized my flying skills and my ability to take control and lead. I was delighted.

CHAPTER 9

QUANG TRI

During the third week of January 1971 we received word that our unit would be moving again. This time it would not be just a short hop from the beach to the airfield. We were going to move our entire unit north, to a town called Quang Tri. Quang Tri was in Northern I Corps, just below the Demilitarized Zone (DMZ).

The U.S. Armed Forces, combined with the ARVN, were mounting a big offensive to push west out to Khe Sanh and into Laos. This would be one of the biggest operations of the entire Vietnam conflict. They were going to move half the country's units north to support this offensive. Lam Son 719 would be the name of the operation. Lam Son had been the birthplace of a famous Vietnamese hero who had defeated the Chinese Army in 1427. The Vietnamese associated the name Lam Son with victory. As for the numbers, the 71 stood for the year 1971, and 9 was the name of the main highway leading out to Khe Sanh.[8] Phase one of this operation, called Dewey Canyon II, would be an American operation to clear Route 9 out to the Laotian border and reopen Khe Sanh.

The purpose of Lam Son 719 was to cut the Ho Chi Minh Trail and to occupy and destroy logistical installations and supplies in base areas 604 and 611 in Laos, thus preventing any NVA offensive into Vietnam for the rest of the year. This would buy time for Vietnamization to work and hopefully convince Hanoi to negotiate.[9] The idea for this offensive came from the successful invasion of Cambodian base areas in May of 1970, which severely disrupted the logistic support of the large Communist forces in central and southern areas of South Vietnam.[10]

Lam Son 719 would change the way the war had been fought since American involvement in Vietnam. After the Cambodian incursion, Congress passed the Cooper-Church Amendment prohibiting American ground troops from entering Cambodia or Laos. This meant that the entire ground assault would be solely ARVN. There would be no American advisors, artillery forward observers, or air controllers on the ground with the ARVN troops when they entered Laos. The United States would provide nearly 10,000 combat, engineering, and support troops, but they were to remain in Quang Tri Province for logistical and combat support, security, and to maintain and arm the helicopters and fixed-wing aircraft. The only U.S. troops that would be participating in Laos would be the pilots.

The tactics used by the North Vietnamese in Lam Son 719 were different from their normal unconventional guerrilla warfare. Due to the overwhelming number of soldiers on their side (approximately two to one), they ended up fighting a much more conventional war. The ARVN started the campaign with 17,000 troops against an estimated 22,000 enemy troops, which in two weeks swelled to nearly 20,000 ARVN and 40,000 North Vietnamese troops.[11] As the ARVN forces pushed west into Laos, they built several fire-support bases, but these isolated bases gave the NVA the opportunity to encircle and destroy them one by one. The NVA tactics were to cut the aerial supply lines with antiaircraft fire and demoralize the ARVN with artillery and mortar barrages around the clock. When ready, and if possible, they would storm the bases with combined infantry and armor forces.[12]

Lam Son 719 was the first time that the helicopter was used in a mid-intensity conflict. The ARVN soldiers were dependent on U.S. helicopter support for insertions and extractions, and for resupply and reconnaissance flights. During Lam Son 719, U.S. helicopters flew ninety thousand sorties, the greatest airmobile support that the United States committed to any one ground campaign during the Vietnam War.[13] The NVA had an estimated 170 to 200 antiaircraft weapons that wreaked havoc on the helicopters. It was a battle like no other ever seen in helicopter warfare.

This campaign would see the largest helicopter assault of the war. On March 6, 120 Huey helicopters lifted the ARVN 2nd and 3rd Battalions of the 2nd Regiment from Khe Sanh to Techepone in a single-ship trail formation, with birds spaced thirty seconds apart in one long column stretching across the horizon.[14] Lam Son 719 also contained the first toe-to-toe armor battle of the Indochina war. Finally, it marked the last offensive operation in which American troops participated, even though it was a supporting role.[15]

Personally, I was not too excited about having to make this move, knowing all the hard work that it would take to get the unit set up again, but as usual I was not asked for my opinion. I had approximately four months left in country, and I would have been perfectly happy to ride them out in a familiar area with a familiar operation. That was not going to happen.

We received orders on January 27, 1971, to have all of our belongings packed and moved to the flight line by the afternoon of the 28th. Even though we had only been in our company area for three months, I felt a lonely feeling come over me as we cleared out our hootchs. I thought that it was rather strange that I would miss the place we had called home for only three months. I also realized that this feeling might have been because we were headed out to who-knows-where. I grabbed my duffle and helmet bag and started walking towards the flight line, wondering what adventures lay ahead. Our briefing had been pretty vague. All we had been told was that we were moving north and details would follow.

Trull and Callahan met me at the flightline. Trull was my bird's crew chief and Callahan was my gunner. They said they had a surprise waiting for me. They took me over to my bird, and a big grin came over my face when I saw my bird. They had the nose cone of my helicopter painted with my call sign, "Rattler One-Seven." Painted between the Rattler and the One-Seven was a big rattlesnake coiled in the attacking position, with horns on it. I loved it. This was one of the best gifts I had ever received. I realized how much my crew respected me, and I, in return, thought a lot of them.

When flight operations assigned 405 (a bird's number as seen on its tail) to me as my personal bird, the tailboom had already been replaced. The new tailboom was covered with zinc chromate to protect it from rusting, but it had never been painted the olive drab green like the rest of the birds. The color of the zinc chromate was much lighter and brighter green than the olive drab green, and it really made my tailboom stick out from the rest of the birds. To help accent this bright green color even more, Trull had waxed the tailboom with some classic car wax, which really made the zinc chromate shine. My crew nicknamed our bird the "Green Lizard."

After all the flightcrews had finished reporting to the flightline, we spent the rest of the afternoon loading the aircraft and briefing for the next day's move. We would stay the night in Chu Lai and start out for Quang Tri on the 29th. The convoy would leave ahead of the flight to arrive at Quang Tri at approximately the same time as we arrived with our birds. Due to bad weather, however, we were not able to complete the flight until January 30.

It was a brisk, chilly morning with a light cloud cover when our flight lifted off from Chu Lai. Our helicopters flew in a trail formation. A feeling of uncertainty lay heavy on our shoulders as we departed, not knowing what to expect from that day forward. Our flight headed north up the Red Ball, a nickname for Highway One, which ran north to south the length of Vietnam. We flew at an altitude of two thousand feet and watched the familiar countryside pass below us. Even though we felt a little apprehensive about the uncertainty of our future, we were still excited, because we knew that this was going to be one of the biggest operations of the Vietnam War and we would be smack in the middle of it.

When our flight reached Da Nang, we swung out towards the beach and headed north along the shoreline. Due to the low clouds, we were forced to slowly descend. Lower and lower we descended until we were 150 feet above the deck. We crossed over the Da Nang Bay and had to swing out over the water because of some steep hills just north of Da Nang. I had never liked flying over the water, and today was no different. Since I never learned how to swim, I felt as if I were playing Russian roulette. There was nothing in our bird that would float, and I knew that if for some unlucky reason our engine quit, which had been known to happen, I would have been just plain out of luck.

The big joke during our briefing was that if we missed Quang Tri, the next stop was Hanoi. We were headed into new country where we had never been before, so we watched our maps closely. Once we got clear of the hills north of Da Nang, our flight headed back inland towards Hue, the scene of much carnage during the Tet Offensive of 1968. As we flew toward Hue, I could not help but think back about what happened there a couple years ago.

Hue had received a lot of attention in the news back in the States during the Tet Offensive of 1968, a turning point in the Vietnam War. Even though we actually won the battles that took place, the political ramifications were disastrous for President Johnson and General Westmoreland. President Johnson's popularity polls dropped from a high of 80% in 1963 down to 30% after the Tet Offensive, and he later decided not to run for re-election. We ended up losing more American lives after Tet than before it.[16]

On the eve of the Lunar New Year, January 31, 1968, NVA Four-Star General Vo Nguyen Giap launched a massive campaign against South Vietnam. Before Tet, the majority of the fighting had been taking place in the rural areas, but this time around the Tet Offensive tactics were to attack urban areas. The NVA earlier attacked the village and Marine firebase at Khe Sanh at dawn on January 21, to draw General Westmoreland's attention away from the cities and to get him to focus his troops on defending Khe Sanh. On the night of January 31, the whole country erupted with attacks. The highland towns of Kon Tum, Pleiku, and Banmethout were simultaneously attacked. The NVA attacked thirteen of the sixteen provincial capitals of the Mekong Delta. In Saigon, the capital of South Vietnam, nineteen Viet Cong sappers attacked the American Embassy and broke through the outer wall of the Embassy compound in less than five minutes. They failed to enter the Embassy itself, however, and by morning all nineteen commandos were dead, along with five Americans and two Vietnamese.

The fights were erupting all over South Vietnam, but the worst battle took place at Hue. Hue was an ancient Vietnamese capital located in Northern I Corps. Ten NVA/Vietcong battalions attacked the city, and within a few hours of fighting, the whole city was overrun except for the U.S. Advisors and the 3rd ARVN Division Headquarters. The enemy's main goal was to capture the Citadel, a gigantic fortress that encompassed approximately two square miles. The enemy captured all but the northeastern section, which was held by some ARVN soldiers. By dawn, the VC flag was flying over the Citadel.

What was to happen next was the horror that humanity sometimes deals out to its own. Once the city and the Citadel were overrun, the NVA began what they called a liberation program. Thousands of prisoners were set free. Then they started rounding up thousands of what they called "enemies of the state" or "enemies of the people," using prepared hit lists. These were political officials, government officials, South Vietnam sympathizers, and Catholics. They rounded these people up into groups and murdered them. Many of the dead found were Catholics who had gone to the churches for sanctuary. The estimated number of civilians missing after the battle of Hue was 5,800. The South Vietnamese uncovered mass graves of almost 1,200 bodies in Hue. Later, they uncovered more mass graves in the provincial area (most likely victims being taken to reeducation camps but murdered when the Americans or ARVN forces got too close), bringing the total massacred close to 2,800 people. With 844 reported killed in the battle, that left more than 2,000 civilians never accounted for and most likely killed.[17] This was the largest communist execution of the war. To my surprise, the antiwar protesters seemed to overlook the atrocities that occurred at Hue.

It took the U.S. Marine and ARVN forces until February 23 to retake the Citadel, and Hue by February 25. It was a tough battle. Some of the Marines that fought at Hue compared it to the urban fighting of World War II, which was very different from the jungle fighting of Vietnam that they were used to. When the battle for Hue was over, the casualties for our side were 119 Americans KIA and 363 ARVN soldiers KIA, compared to an estimated 7,000 NVA KIA. As I looked over the now peaceful city of Hue, it was hard to believe that such a battle ever took place.[18]

Upon reaching Hue, our flight picked up Highway One again. As we proceeded further north, we could see the weather changing. It was the monsoon season for this part of the country—the temperature was turning colder and the skies were getting cloudier. Highway One took us right into Quang Tri. The countryside around Quang Tri was quite different from what we were used to at Chu Lai. The lay of the land was a lot flatter than our old AO, with little foliage and a lack of contour that gave it an open feeling. A large, flat plain with very few trees and a lot of tall elephant grass ran from the beach inland for several miles, before reaching the mountains.

Upon reaching Quang Tri, our flight was directed to land at a barren open field south of the main airstrip. While we were on final approach to this field, I scanned across the area and noticed nothing there, no man-made structures. After we landed, we were told to shut our engines down, so we did and secured the birds. We then met with our company commander, who informed us that this would be our new home. We were all surprised, because there was nothing there. No buildings, no water, and no supplies, just sand and weeds. I could tell that the men—including me—were not in the mood for sleeping in a cold, wet field.

We hunted up some C-Rations for lunch and then set out to retrieve some cots for sleeping. We did not want to sleep on the wet ground if we could help it. I cranked up our bird and headed for the 101st for help. We knew that they could give us assistance, being within their area of operation. We spent the afternoon flying around trying to locate the proper materials and equipment that we were assigned to pick up. As soon as we completed our mission, we headed back to our new home. The sun was setting when Quang Tri appeared on the horizon. It had been a long day, and we were expecting an even longer night. When we returned, I was surprised at how the company area had been transformed. It was starting to look a little more like it should. The convoy had arrived and the men had been working hard to set up the equipment. They had the operations tent, the mess tent, and a few others set up and were busy working on the rest. What a difference a few hours made.

About a half-mile north of our field, our men found a couple of old sheds for the pilots' sleeping quarters. A Holiday Inn it was not, but they certainly would help keep the wind and rain out. Up to this point in my tour, I had not experienced any extremely cold weather in Nam, but that night I did. Even though I was snuggled in my mummy bag with my socks on, my toes were still cold. It somewhat reminded me of my home in Minnesota. The temperature must have hit in the low thirties during the night, but with all the moisture and humidity from the rainy season, it seemed much colder. Thank God we were not sleeping on the wet ground.

When morning came, we dragged our warm bodies out from our bags into that damp, cold air. We spent the second day at Quang Tri scouting around for specific types of supplies and equipment, in order to get our company area organized. In the early evening, we received a flight briefing for the following day. Some of the SACs were assigned to fly with the 101st pilots. Since it was their area of operation, they would be able to give us a good orientation. I was excited. I thought it would be interesting to see how the other helicopter units operated, compared to ours. After the briefing was over, we returned to our new quarters and tried to make the best of what we had. Someone had already located a generator and set it up and had it running. At least we had some lights, and just having that made our new home appear warmer and more livable. I hit my sleeping bag early and tried to rest up for the next day.

Morning came fast and early with a damp, cold chill in the air. It was still dark when I rolled out of my bag and got dressed. We had about a half-mile walk to the company area. We walked along the sandy, damp tracks that the vehicles had cut in the field. Our boots got quite wet and were covered with sand by the time we arrived at our company area. The cooks were just beginning to mill around in the mess tent trying to round up some breakfast. I made a quick stop at the latrine and then went over to the mess tent to pick up a little breakfast, just some bread and bacon. I had never been very big on eating breakfast, and just looking at our mess personnel and their sloppy appearance reinforced this belief. After breakfast, we walked over to operations, received the final briefing for the day, and headed toward the aircraft.

The day's flying with the 101st turned out to be very interesting. The first thing I learned was that the 101st's idea of low-level flying was entirely different from ours. Our technique was to fly the bird as low as we could safely fly without hitting the trees or surface, and to S-turn back and forth utilizing the trees and foliage for cover. Their idea was to fly in a somewhat straight line about fifteen to twenty feet above the trees or surface. Throughout the day, I felt like a sitting duck flying that high. The AC with whom I was flying gave me an excellent orientation of the area, showing me the locations of their different fire-support bases. He also explained where the safe areas were and pointed out where "no-man's-land" was located.

In our old AO, our primary enemy was the Viet Cong, but up here, our enemy was the NVA, who fought a different type of warfare. What had been a safe way of flying in our AO was not necessarily a safe way to fly here, and vice versa. For example, in our old AO, one of the worst things you could do was fly low-level down the rivers and streams. Sure enough, there we were flying low-level right down a river heading back to Quang Tri. I felt very uneasy, even though the AC assured me that they did this all the time. The river we were following wound through the flat, grassy plain situated between the sea and the mountains to the west. The AC told me, "The NVA are smart enough not to get caught out here in the open, and since there aren't too many VC around, it's rather safe." I still felt uncomfortable, but I understood that when in Rome, do as the Romans do, so I listened carefully. Tomorrow I would take one of our unit's pilots out, one who had not flown today, and give him the same orientation.

When I returned home, I noticed several more changes since I had left that morning. The company area was really taking shape. One of the major problems we encountered early when parking the birds was that every time an aircraft came in to land, it would end up dusting everyone off because of the large amounts of sand in the fields. When I got back to the hootchs, I noticed that the guys who had not flown had really done a lot of work on them. They had patched up the holes in the ceiling and walls and had inserted new walls between our cots, giving almost everyone individual cubicles. They had also lined up some hootch maids, though I would not get to see them until I got a day down from flying.

We spent the next couple of days giving our pilots orientation flights. We were also flying and supporting the ground forces as they worked their way towards Khe Sanh, an area heavy with combat in previous years. Khe Sanh had been a U.S. Special Forces base for years and a Marine fire base back in the sixties. At Khe Sanh the Marines fought what were called the "Hill Fights" from April 24 through early May of 1967, losing approximately 160 men with another 440 wounded in action and 2 missing in action. The Marines confirmed 807 NVA dead, with another 611 KIAs probable, and 6 POWs. The following year, from January 21 through April 14, 1968, Khe Sanh was besieged during the Tet Offensive.[19]

The reason we were pushing back out to Khe Sanh was that it was going to be used as the focal point for all their activities during this operation. The airstrip, which had been deserted for a few years, would accommodate C-130 transports. It was also close to the Laotian border, and the ARVN was planning a big push into Laos. Khe Sanh was situated on a high plateau with a high ridgeline to the north and mountains to the west. It was an opening in the rugged mountains that formed a boundary between South Vietnam and Laos, known in Vietnam as the D'Ai Lao. The countryside surrounding Khe Sanh was very beautiful. The old abandoned airstrip was located in the middle of the

15. A photo taken along Route 9 on the way to Khe Sanh in the vicinity of LZ Vandergrift. This area was known as the rock pile. (Photo courtesy of Don Lynam.)

plateau, and it was in this area that the U.S. and ARVN forces chose to base their camps in order to take advantage of the airstrip.

For my first mission, I was assigned to work with some officers from the U.S. Army Corps of Engineers. They were in charge of cutting out a new road to lead to Khe Sanh from the north. This area was extremely hilly and wooded, so being able to survey the land from the air was very helpful to them. Because of the hilly terrain, the engineers would have to wind the road a lot to work its way around the hills, so that it could be usable to the troops. It was imperative that our troops had two land routes out of Khe Sanh. While flying over this mountainous terrain we tried to survey the best route for a back door to Khe Sanh. I could see that it would be easy to conceal any troops' movements, because of the denseness of the foliage. But once they cut this road out of the jungle, I wondered how they would be able to keep it open and secure?

The other route leading to Khe Sanh was QL 9, also known as Route 9. It started at Dong Ha, the city just north of Quang Tri, and headed west through Cam Lo. At Thon Son Lam it swung south for about eight clicks, then back southwest running along the north side of the river, De Quang Tri, for nine clicks. It continued out past Khe Sanh into Laos. As Route 9 swung back toward Khe Sanh, it became just a dusty, dirt trail leading approximately three clicks south of the airstrip and continuing on into Laos. All the ground troops and vehicles carrying the supplies would be taking this route, so it was very important to secure the entire valley along this route leading to Khe Sanh.

We could tell that this operation was going to be bigger than any other operation that we had seen. Daily, more and more troops and supplies were coming up from the South. There were more helicopters than I had ever seen, hundreds of them. Flying reconnaissance along Highway One and Route 9 (QL 9), I could see the convoys stretching from one horizon to the other. It was quite impressive. I had never seen anything like this before. There were tanks, armored personnel carriers (APCs), deuce-and-a-halfs, field artillery, and jeeps. Everything that you could possibly imagine in a military convoy was down on the road headed west toward Khe Sanh. As I flew over this massive convoy, I thought to myself, "This is what World War II must have looked like." It did not take a whole lot of imagination to realize that the enemy could not possibly miss seeing all the activity. They would know we were coming.

CHAPTER 10

RANK

As the push to Khe Sanh continued, our unit continued flying several types of missions, ranging from resupply and combat assaults to troop insertions and extractions. We flew a lot of reconnaissance work, but sometimes we were stuck flying what I called taxi service. Taxi service normally consisted of ferrying the senior ranking officers from the brigades that we were supporting out to different sites in the field. We would wait while they held their conferences and then fly them back to headquarters—hence the nickname for such boring flying.

Most of the officers we ran this taxi service for were great to work with, but there were always a few ants in the picnic basket. From my own experiences, I soon discovered that if you were working with a full bird colonel, who knew that he did not stand a chance of making general, then you were almost guaranteed that he would be great to fly for. He was not there to impress his superiors and win medals, he just wanted to do a good job and get his mission accomplished. But if we were flying for someone who stood the slightest chance of making general, look out! He would most likely be a Patton-in-disguise. Several of the lieutenant colonels who were pushing to make full bird colonel carried this same asshole trait in their character.

We were taught in flight school that the aircraft commander was in charge of and responsible for the aircraft and the lives of the crew and its occupants. The AC was the ultimate commander of the aircraft, no matter who was on board or who we were flying support for, because as an AC we knew and understood the mission and the limitations of the helicopter much better than the officer accompanying us did. The majority of the officers we supported were not aviation-rated and

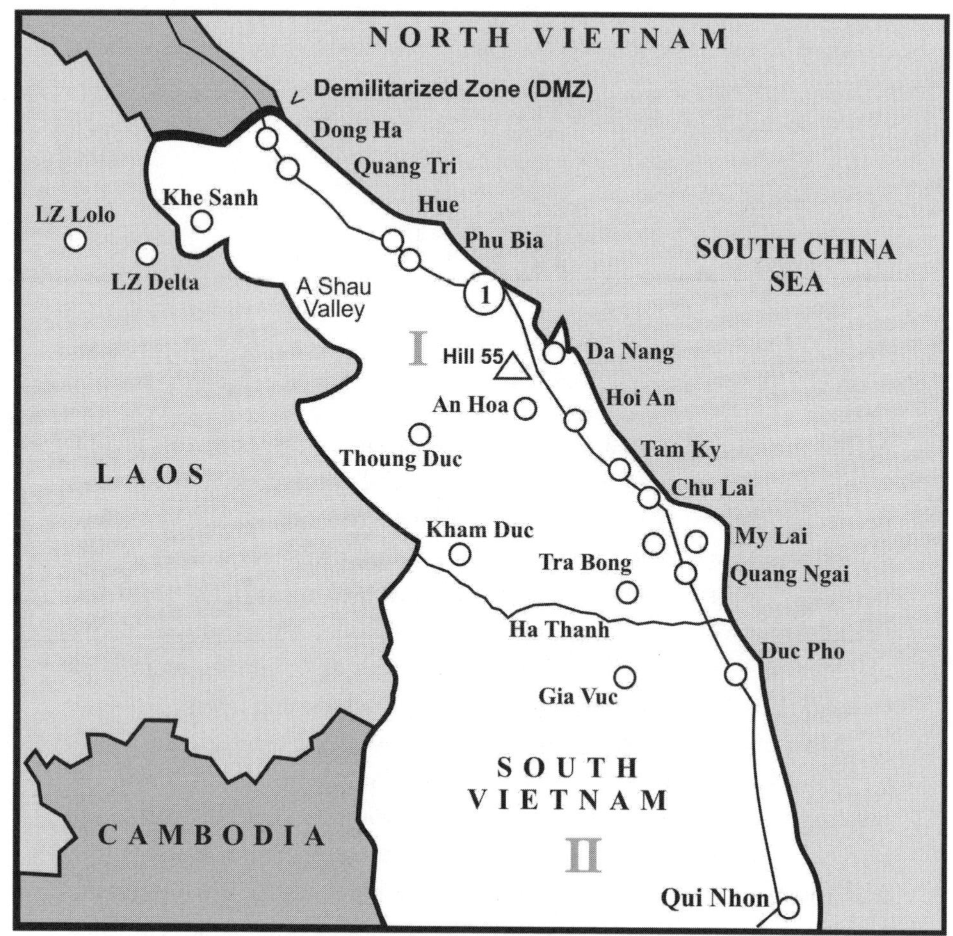

16. Map of I Corps, showing the location of Chu Lai and Quang Tri. The map also shows the locations of LZ Delta and LZ Lolo in Laos.

therefore had a very limited understanding of the actual fundamentals of helicopter flight. For instance, if we were assigned to work with a colonel, he would most likely be an infantry, artillery, or maybe even an armor officer. That would be his area of expertise, not aviation. He might order us to do something with our aircraft that we felt the helicopter could not do. If this happened, we could and should refuse to obey his order. However, if we did refuse to obey his order, we had better be sure that we were right. That was the tricky part, being sure that you were right.

This happened to me on two occasions while flying out at Khe Sanh. The first incident occurred early one morning when I was assigned to fly a colonel and two majors, from one of the infantry brigades temporarily based at Quang Tri out to Khe Sanh. Our mission was very simple. Our orders were to fly the officers out to Khe Sanh, wait while they accomplished their business, and then return them to Quang Tri.

It was one of those damp, drizzly mornings when we set our chopper down at headquarters. The clouds were just barely hovering over the ridgelines, blocking the rays from the morning sun and limiting our forward visibility for flight. As I rolled the throttle back, I could see out of the corner of my eye the colonel and his two majors as they walked out to the aircraft and climbed in. Once the officers were inside the chopper, one of the majors gave us the thumbs up. I rolled the throttle back up, and we lifted off.

We took off low-leveling across the grassy plains, staying clear of the clouds that appeared to hang just inches above our spinning rotor. I pointed the ship west and we headed off towards Khe Sanh, flying due west until we picked up Route 9. We then turned and low-leveled along Route 9, which paralleled a small river, until the point where the river veered northwest, and the road swung southwest. At this split, we swung northwest following the river, which led out toward Khe Sanh, and continued until it ran directly into the side of a mountain. At the junction of where the river ran into the side of the mountain hung a waterfall. As we approached the waterfall, I cyclic climbed the helicopter up the side of the waterfall. (A cyclic climb is a climbing maneuver where you trade the forward airspeed of the bird by pulling back on the cyclic for a quick altitude gain.) Performing a cyclic climb was always a fun maneuver to perform, because as the helicopter rapidly climbed upward, it gave you an exhilarating feeling of freedom. You felt as if you had broken free from the earth's pull of gravity, and to do it right in front of a mountainside with the waterfall appearing between the center of your legs (as viewed through the bird's chin bubble) was a fantastic feeling. Once we got on top of the ridgeline, we followed the stream at the top of the falls for about a kilometer, which took us right into Khe Sanh. After setting the bird down at Khe Sanh, one of the majors came over and said, "Thanks for the ride, I really enjoyed it, but I don't think the colonel cared for it too much."

After approximately forty-five minutes, the officers reappeared at the chopper for their flight back to Quang Tri. I rapidly cranked up the Huey as they climbed aboard. I carefully lifted the chopper to a hover, and then did a pedal turn into the wind. I nosed the cyclic forward as our chopper gained altitude and headed back low-level across the trees toward the waterfall. When we came to the edge of the mountain, we descended down the falls to the stream below and started following the river back towards Route 9. As we were low-leveling down the river, I got a call over the intercom from my crew chief, Trull, who was sitting behind the colonel. He passed on an order from the colonel to get off the deck, meaning for me to stop low-leveling. I responded with a chuckle, "He can't do that!" But Trull insisted that the colonel was dead serious. So I told Trull, "Explain to the colonel that it is our company's SOP [standard operating procedure] that if the ceiling is less than 1500 feet, we are required to fly low-level for tactical reasons." Trull tried explaining this to the colonel, but the colonel said he did not care and told me, through Trull, "It's a direct order—get off the deck now!"

It appeared that the colonel did not like low-level flying, and now he wanted me to risk the lives of my crew, the other officers, and his own, just so that he could feel better. I thought to myself, "This direct order is absurd, but I need to do something," so I immediately pulled back on the cyclic and popped the aircraft up into a rapid vertical climb. The helicopter shot up like a rocket headed for outer space until we hit the base of the clouds, which were at approximately 500 feet above the ground. There, I leveled off, flew for a few seconds in the clouds, and then descended the bird back down to the deck, where I continued to low-level back towards Quang Tri. I told Trull, "You tell the colonel that the ceiling is 500 feet, and we require a 1500 foot ceiling not to low-level." I knew that for us to fly down that river at 450 feet above the ground would be suicidal—shooting at a Huey at 450 feet is like shooting at a barn, with plenty of time for the enemy to locate you, put you in their sites, and get off several shots. Flying low-level, your exposure to the enemy is so much less because by the time they see you, you are out of sight. I knew it was safe to fly at a higher altitude back towards the coast, where there was minimal enemy contact, but we were not back along the coast—we were way out by Khe Sanh. When we arrived back at Quang Tri, the colonel stormed off without saying a word. I guess he was not used to people disobeying his orders, but at least the two majors took the time to thank us.

I was assigned to fly resupply when the second occurrence happened. It was mid-morning, and the ceiling was hanging low with the clouds nestled on top of the ridgelines again. The major that I was working for had an outpost located on top of one of the ridgelines just northwest of our ground position. This outpost was actively engaged in combat with the enemy and in need of resupply. The major called me over and explained that I needed to load my Huey with supplies and drop them off at the unit's location on the ridge. As he talked, I could see the outpost and knew that the ceiling was too low to accomplish the mission. When he finished speaking, I tried to explain to him, "The outpost that you want me to resupply is socked in. The weather is too bad, and we need to wait for the ceiling to lift before we can get our bird into their LZ." After listening to me, the major got on the radio and called his unit. They told the major that they had no problem seeing down the valley to our location. Of course they could see us, but this did not change the fact that the clouds were still hovering over their heads. This so-called "weather report" was good enough for the major, and he immediately ordered me to complete the mission. I again tried to explain to him, "You can't take a Huey, fill it full with supplies, and just hover up the side of the mountain, especially over enemy troops that we know are there. We'll be shot down. Furthermore, we have to have altitude above the LZ to be able to shoot an approach into the LZ. We can't shoot an approach from below the LZ. It just can't physically be done!" As usual, the major would not accept no for an answer.

I wanted to accomplish this mission and resupply the men as badly as the major did, but I wasn't going to risk my aircraft or my crew to accomplish it. But being good soldiers, we had to give it a try. We loaded the supplies into our bird and departed. As we lifted off from our pad, I thought to myself, "What a waste of time and expense to takeoff, knowing that it is impossible to complete the task that we are assigned." Within minutes, we were setting back down on the pad with the supplies still on board. I again explained to the major that what he was asking us to do could not possibly be done until the ceiling lifted. The major was not happy to hear this, but I think he realized that he had no other choice. (Fortunately for the troops, by the end of the day the weather had lifted enough that we could resupply them.)

I found this type of officer very frustrating to work under. I never could understand why some officers were like that. It always made sense to me to believe the experts. If my crew chief came to me and told me that the bird was unsafe to fly because of a mechanical problem, I would certainly believe him.

Right before our company moved up to Quang Tri, we had several new officers assigned to our unit. One of the new pilots was a captain who was assigned to our platoon and was to become our platoon leader. His name was Captain Randall (I have changed the name for reasons that will become obvious). Captain Randall was a large man, very thick and solid in stature. When he began flying with us out at Khe Sanh, he tended to intimidate some of our newer warrant officer ACs because of his size, his personality, or maybe because he was a captain. One afternoon, a couple of warrant officers approached me. They were very upset and were complaining about Randall's conduct when they had flown with him. They told me that he would just take over command of their ship, and that they were not sure how to handle him. They had never had this happen to them before, and I could tell as I listened to their story that it was definitely stressing them out. They went on to explain how Randall would climb into their ship and then physically take over the controls from them rather than waiting until he was told to fly. They thought that since I was an SAC, that maybe I could possibly help them. I told them, "Let him fly with me, and we'll see what happens." I knew that it would not be long before I flew with him because he was in First Platoon. I neither knew Captain Randall, nor had I talked to him much before we flew together, but just the thought that he or anyone would just take the controls from an aircraft commander appalled me. In the army, the aircraft commander has full authority over everyone on his aircraft regardless of rank. This was a pillar of Army Aviation. It took a lot of hard work and experience to become an AC, and to have some new pilot disregard and disrespect the position made me fume. I thought to myself, "We'll see."

Within a few days we were scheduled to fly together. We met down at the flight line and performed our preflight duties as usual. We then climbed into our bird, and I flew her up to the unit that we were assigned to support that morning. Sure enough, when it came time for us to take off on our first assignment, Captain Randall got on the controls, even though I was already on them, and attempted to lift our bird to a hover. I was ready. I immediately yelled, "What are you doing? I've got the aircraft. You don't touch the controls unless I tell you to fly!" Then I took control of the bird from him and proceeded to fly the next five or six sorties. I did this to make sure that he got a clear picture, that it was the AC who was in charge of the aircraft, not the highest-ranking officer. I knew that he already knew this, but I felt that after the way he had been acting with the newer ACs, it would not hurt to reinforce it.

Later that morning when we had a break in our flying, I told Randall how several of the newer ACs had been complaining about him. I explained to him how he had been taking away their authority by taking over the controls and trying to run the ship. I emphasized that he must understand that even though he was a captain and they were warrant officers that while he was flying in their aircraft, they actually outranked him, because they were the AC. I told him, "The AC is the one who is responsible for command of the ship, period." He listened and seemed to understand the message that I was trying to get across. We then spent the rest of the day with us both flying and discussing flying techniques.

A few days later, I was flying support for an infantry unit located west of Khe Sanh, out towards the Laotian border. I had a lieutenant from operations as my copilot. He was our administration officer, whose job was to shuffle papers and do the administrative work for our company, so he had not done a lot of flying out in our AO. Because of the reduction of American forces being sent to Vietnam, the 71st was starting to get short on pilots, and so he would be filling in more and more for us as the months went by. We spent most of the day flying single ship (by ourselves), carrying supplies to the ground units that we were supporting. These units' positions were located in the mountain country southwest of Khe Sanh.

The winds had been blowing strong all day, making the flying strenuous and tiring. All morning and into the afternoon, we had been shooting high overhead approaches into our units' positions. At about 1600 hours we received a radio call. One of the ground units had just declared a tactical emergency. Because of the intense fighting with Charlie going on at their position, they were running low on ammunition and needed to be resupplied before nightfall, or else they would not make it through the night. We immediately loaded up our bird with ammunition and C-rations and then headed out to their location. Before long it would be getting dark. We had flown into their location earlier in the afternoon, so we knew where they were.

As soon as we arrived over their location, I tried to raise radio contact with the unit, but no one answered. We could tell by our visual observation that the unit was in the middle of an intense firefight and evidently they could not afford the manpower to have someone man the radio. We kept circling, trying to raise contact without success. The clock kept ticking, stealing with every sweep of its hand the precious minutes that we needed before sunset and its black glove of darkness that would engulf us. As I watched the sun hit the horizon, I knew that it was time to make a quick decision. I had two choices: leave without resupplying the unit, which would surely mean death; or go into the location without radio contact. I chose the second.

Without having the smoke to determine the wind direction and its strength, I decided to set up for our approach in the same direction as when we had landed there a few hours earlier. I executed a high overhead approach but as I rolled out on short final, it became apparent that it was extremely windy, and the wind had worked its way around into a cornering tailwind. I tried to flare the bird and pulled pitch to bring the bird to a hover, but due to the gusty winds blowing up our tail she would not respond. It was as if the movements of my controls did not matter. The bird would not stop and kept coming down, headed for the ground. I was beginning to lose control. With our heavy load of ammunition combined with the strong gusty winds, I had no choice but to overtorque the bird and bring in more power than what we were allowed by our engine limitations, or else we would crash into the ground. I pulled what power it took to stop us from hitting the ground. As I pulled power, I ran out of left pedal authority due to the strong winds and the application of power, and the helicopter began to spin out of control. Around we spun until the aircraft stabilized in the direction of the wind. What a wild ride the last few seconds had been, but I finally had the bird stabilized in a hover. I immediately set the chopper down. My crew and a few ground soldiers quickly unloaded the ammunition from our bird as the firefight continued around us. With all the shooting going on, we had to get out of there quickly. I pulled pitch, and we exited the LZ as fast as we had entered.

The sun was disappearing below the horizon as we flew our wounded bird home. We radioed in to maintenance to report that we had overtorqued our bird (they would have to ground the aircraft for a maintenance inspection due to the overtorque). They would first pull the chip detectors to check them for small metal shavings, which would indicate that the transmission had been overstressed by the application of the additional power. This could possibly take the bird out of service. I was upset. I had never overtorqued an aircraft before and had thought I never would. When someone overtorqued a bird, it was usually because of pilot error. I also knew, however, that I could not leave that unit out in the field, knowing that they were running out of ammunition. I had made my decision, and I would live with it.

Fortunately, I had been flying with the admin officer that day. As soon as we arrived back at our unit, Captain Kaiser (name changed to protect the guilty), our company commander, met us at the flight line ranting and raving about the overtorque and saying that he was going to put me up on charges. After Captain Kaiser finished his yelling and screaming, the admin officer softly but forcefully told Kaiser, "If anything is to be done, you should put Gross up for a medal. If he hadn't done what he did, a lot of lives would have been lost." After hearing the lieutenant's statement, Fast Teddy (the nickname most of the men in the unit called Captain Kaiser) decided to drop the charges.

To make matters even worse, when I arrived back at the company area, a couple of pilots came over and told me that Captain Randall had been talking me down. He had been telling everyone that he had just flown with me a few days earlier and did not like the way I flew. He was telling them that he had told me I had been shooting my approaches too steep and fast, and this would one day get me into trouble. Thank goodness these pilots had flown with me and knew that

I did not fly that way. That was exactly what I had told Randall not to do. He had taken my words and turned them around. Hearing these lies, I grew hot. I asked the men, "Where is Randall now?" They pointed me towards one of the hootchs. Furious, I immediately headed toward the hootch. I guess this was his way of getting back at me for our little discussion on him taking over control of the aircraft from the other ACs. I did not care if he was a captain and now my platoon leader, he was an asshole and that had to be corrected.

Randall outweighed me by a good thirty pounds and was at least an inch or two taller than I, and I knew that he could probably tear me apart, but I did not care. I would not allow people to tell lies about my flying, especially after what had just happened. I stormed into the hootch and told Randall that I wanted to talk to him outside in private. We both walked out of the hootch over to an open area between the hootchs. I turned and asked him, "What the hell are you telling theses guys about my flying? You weren't there, so you have no way of knowing what happened." I was expecting a big confrontation and was ready to go to it. But to my surprise, he apologized and said he was sorry. I was shocked! What could I do but accept his apology. I turned and walked back to my hootch. It had been a hell of a day, and I needed some rest.

Fast Teddy was a different story. He had come to our company in late December to replace Maj. Myron Davis as our new company commander. Whereas before, we always had a major as our CO, now we had a captain. This was unusual in an aviation company, for more than half of our pilots were commissioned officers, and we had several captains. Fast Teddy was to become the worst CO that I had ever had.

When he first came to our company, he called the officers together and spoke. We could tell right away by his foul language and mannerisms that his attitude was going to be different from that of our other COs. I knew right away that he was going to be a hard CO to get along with and work under. Fast Teddy had come up through the ranks as an enlisted man for several years before becoming an officer, and it showed. He spoke to his officers as if they were enlisted men, showing no respect. He would cuss and swear at us like a drill sergeant shouting at his trainees during boot camp. What a change this would be. Fast

Teddy would do more to destroy the morale of the Rattlers than anything throughout my entire Vietnam tour. Instead of getting his men to work for him as a good leader does, he had a way of making the men work against him. A book, in itself, could be written just about Fast Teddy's antics. Unfortunately for us, Captain "Fast Teddy" Kaiser would be our company commander during Lam Son 719.

CHAPTER 11

LAM SON 719

February 2, 1971

Dear Tom,

Hi and how is everyone? I'm sorry I didn't write sooner. We're in the middle of a big operation and I just don't have the time. We moved out of Chu Lai and are up north along the DMZ, now working the Khe Sanh Valley. We are presently living in Quang Tri and it's a lot worse than Chu Lai. We're operating our company out of tents and that's really bad for the maintenance of our aircraft. We have no place to take a shower now and I think that's the worst part. I imagine you'll be reading about this operation in the newspaper and on TV. It's one of the biggest in the war. You won't believe how cold it is here! I got Mother's letter of the 25th tonight. I really appreciate hearing from you all.

Today I go under 100 days left in country. I'm really anxious to leave. It just all builds up on you after awhile.

We left Chu Lai on the morning of January 30 and arrived at Quang Tri that afternoon. From February 1–7 we were involved in support of Operation Dewey Canyon II, the first phase of Lam Son 719. By February 8, the ARVN forces had already re-established the airstrip at Khe Sanh and had secured the surrounding area along Route 9 and Khe Sanh. Officially, Lam Son 719 started at 1000 hours on February 8th when the ARVN 1st Armored Brigade crossed into Laos. [20]

The helicopter would play a major part in this operation. By the time Lam Son 719 was over, there would be more than 107 helicopters lost and several hundred more shot up. In our company during this campaign, every one of our slicks would be shot down or shot up so bad that it would have to be taken out of service for at least a day to be repaired. It was to be a war like no other we had seen.

There were hundreds of army helicopters supporting the different ARVN units. There were the Rattlers and the Firebirds, along with the Kingsmen, the Redskins, the BlackWidows, the Hawks, the Dolphins, the Sharks, the Phoenixes, the Pachyderms, and many others.[21] These were the names of the units' regular call signs, but for security reasons the higher-ups changed all our call signs. Our new call sign was Benign Fires.

Every pilot in our company had a different perspective of Lam Son 719 depending on what he saw and experienced. He formed his perspective based on which days he flew, which missions he was assigned to, and which position his bird occupied in the flight formation during the combat assaults. He would have an entirely different experience as Chalk One than he would further back as Chalk Twenty-five. It seemed that the closer you were toward the front of the formation, the worse experience you would have for that particular mission.

Up to this point in my tour, excluding the special mission for which I had volunteered, it had been a routine tour. We would periodically get shot at and take a few hits, but it was not happening every day. We could go several days without even being fired upon. That changed with Lam Son 719.

Just as we were starting to get comfortable in our new shacks, headquarters decided to move our company area over toward the western boundary of Quang Tri, to the old dog compound. We were never told why we had to move, but I believe it was because it was too sandy where we had initially set up on the south end of the airstrip. The crews could not keep the sand out of the aircraft engines, and it was wreaking havoc on the rotor blades and control linkages of our aircraft.

A few nights earlier, I was returning to the flight line from my day's flying to park the bird. It was getting dark and time to call it quits for the day. While shooting my approach to our parking spot, I noticed that another one of our birds had come in a few minutes before us. Their crew was busy cleaning their sand separator and getting their bird ready for the night. I had no choice but to hover my bird over and set it down in its proper place. I knew this would dust this crew off, because the flight line was too sandy for helicopter operations, but it was beyond my control. I hated having to dust someone off, knowing I could do nothing to avoid it. Then to make matters worse, one of the pilots of the other bird, who just happened to be a captain from the second platoon, came striding over to give me a hard time. I told him that I was sorry and explained to him about the sandy flight line. I knew that he understood, but my explanation and apology was not good enough for him. He just went on and on, chewing me out. Captain or no captain he finally made me so mad that I told him, "Don't ever bawl me out in front of my crew again. If you want to talk to me, you can talk to me in a reasonable manner or else wait until we're alone, but don't ever chew me out in front of my crew." This was one of my first confrontations with a pilot of higher rank, who most likely felt he had authority over me because of his higher rank. He was a newer pilot to our unit, and I had not flown or worked with him yet. More and more, our company was losing warrant officers, and they were being replaced with commissioned officers. This was a bad move, I felt, on the part of the army.

As we moved to our new company area, I could tell right away that this had been a good location decision. It was going to be a little nicer. The guys got together and built a shower. Since we were always getting dusted off, it would be nice to be able to wash all the sand and red dust off. In this new area, we had regular hootchs again. They were a lot like the ones that we had back on the beach at Chu Lai, except the new ones had no partitions in them. There were bunkers that were spaced between some of the hootchs, and they would come in handy during the rocket and mortar attacks.

During the first days of Lam Son 719, we flew a lot of resupply and insertions. One day we were scheduled to fly in a massive troop movement of ARVN soldiers over into Laos. Early in the morning, we cranked up our flight of birds and headed out to Khe Sanh. The weather was overcast but the ceiling was high enough that we did not have to low-level. We would be joining up with several other units

17. Aircraft parked at Quang Tri in the dirt and sand. This sand wreaked havoc on the birds and made them more difficult to maintain. (Photo courtesy of Don Lynam.)

once we arrived at Khe Sanh. As our formation shot our approach into Khe Sanh, we could see several other birds already parked along the side of the runway.

At approximately 1000 hrs, we loaded up our ARVN troops and cranked up our birds. We would not be leading the formation. Instead, our unit was located towards the middle, with chalk numbers in the high forties and fifties. Once all the troops were loaded, the massive formation lifted off from the Khe Sanh airstrip and headed southwest towards Laos. I am sure this had to be one of the largest helicopter formations of all time. The formation had close to a hundred birds in it.

Right from the start the insertion had problems in the LZ. The LZ was hot and not as secure as they had anticipated. The air mission commander sent over half the formation off to the east to hold in a holding pattern. We were unable to see the LZ from where we were circling, but we could listen to the action taking place on our radio. It sounded like one big screw up. The first ships going in to the LZ started taking hits and were either shot down or had to abort their approach, due to the intensive fire. All we could do was to continue to circle and listen. Sitting there listening to the action, but not actually being involved in it, was the hardest part of combat flying. I felt my stomach tighten as we listened to the action. Finally, the command and control (C&C) ship decided to send the remainder of the flight back to Khe Sanh for more fuel, which allowed time to call in air strikes around the perimeter of the LZ. We understood that with all the downed ships in the LZ, there was no room left to safely set down any other helicopters. My crew and I felt a sigh of relief as we returned to Khe Sanh for more fuel.

Back at Khe Sanh, we immediately refueled and then grabbed some C-rations for lunch. As we sat there in our bird eating lunch, I decided to ask my crew, "What do you want me to do if we go down, and you end up getting pinned under the bird and we can't get you out? Do you want me to shoot you or let the NVA get you?" They looked at me as if I were deranged! What kind of question was that, they wondered? While we had been circling, listening to all the action taking place, I was reminded of our special mission on August 15 and thought it would be a good idea to know, in advance, what my crew members preferred. I told them, "If I'm trapped and cannot get free or if I'm knocked unconscious and you can't get me out, I want you to go ahead and kill me rather than let the gooks get a hold of me." As I spoke, I could tell by the reaction on my crew's faces that they really did not want to think about this possibility. My crew probably thought that I was a little crazy, but I had thought it would be nice to know their wishes.

Back in our old area of operations, we had been told that if a VC shot down a helicopter, he received a reward. They would get to take an R&R to Paris. Also in our old AO, they did not keep helicopter pilots as prisoners for long. The Viet Cong (or more likely North Vietnamese regulars at this time in the war, as I learned later), truly hated the helicopter, and they would take this hatred out on its pilots and crew members. One of our sister company birds had been shot down and part of the crew was captured. We heard from the locals that Charlie paraded the pilots around in tiger cages. They lugged them through the local villages for a couple of nights for propaganda, and then executed them. My biggest fear, more so than dying, was to crash and get knocked unconscious and wake up with a bunch of gooks standing over me.

We finished our C-rations and waited for our mission to resume. Within the hour they had us back in the air headed to Laos. We ended up making our insertion into the LZ that afternoon without taking any casualties.

One night we had a little excitement, back home in our company area. As I had mentioned earlier, Captain Kaiser was not well liked by his troops. I was lying in my cot when I heard someone discharge a clip from an M16. We heard a large commotion taking place outside the headquarters hootch. One of the enlisted men decided that he had had enough of Fast Teddy. He walked into Fast Teddy's office and unloaded a clip of rounds from his M16 directly at him. By some miracle (if you want to call it that) he missed and Kaiser got by without even a scratch. How he missed we will never know, and I confess my first thought was, "Too bad." Maybe he had just been trying to scare Fast Teddy, or more likely he was so loaded that he could not shoot straight. Who knows?

Kaiser came unglued. He called the whole company out in formation and started yelling and screaming, "I'm not going to allow the enlisted men to have weapons in the company area anymore." I thought, "That's really smart!" There we were, out in a combat zone, located along the outside perimeter of the compound, and he will not allow the men to have weapons. Smart, real smart. The scariest thing was that he was serious. Good old Kaiser. Thank goodness, someone turned him in to the higher-ups and the weapons issue was resolved.

Every night Charlie was launching rockets into our base camp. It always seemed to happen just about the time that I fell asleep. A loud high-pitched whistle, followed by an earthshaking explosion, would rock us from our sleep. The first few nights, we all scrambled to the bunkers between the hootchs. A bunch of men huddling in a bunker in their shorts was not a pretty sight. But as the rocket attacks continued nightly, we decided that it was better to get our sleep than huddle in the bunker all night. By the end of the week, only the short timers were getting up and running to the bunker. The rest of us just rolled over and went back to sleep. Otherwise we would not have gotten any rest.

My flight records show that we were doing a lot of flying. On the 9th, I flew 10.5 hours; on the 10th, 9.3 hours; on the 11th, 5.3 hours; on the 12th, 10.1 hours; on the 13th, 6.6 hours; and on the 14th, 5.8 hours. That was 47.6 hours in five days. Would the flying let up? It did not—on the 17th, I got 10.8 hours; on the 18th, 8.3 hours; on the 19th, 9.0 hours; on the 21st, 9.8 hours; on the 22nd, 9.8 hours; and on the 24th, 11.3 hours. All we did was fly and sleep. That amount of flying would continue until the end of March, and it was only mid-February.

There was never a dull moment. Someone was always getting shot down or his aircraft would get so shot up that it was no longer flyable. This had to be the helicopter battle of all time. Our adrenaline was flowing twenty-four hours a day. One morning, I was leading a flight into one of the numerous outposts into which we had been flying. There were several: LZ Bravo, LZ Hotel, LZ Hope, LZ Sophia, LZ Liz, LZ Lolo, LZ Saigon, LZ Yellow, LZ Blue, etc. There were a lot of landing zones and a lot of missions. LZ Sophia, LZ Liz, and LZ Lolo were named after the movie stars Sophia Loren, Elizabeth Taylor, and Gina Lolobrigida.

I was flight lead one morning and had a new copilot on board. He had just come up from the south. As we started our approach into the LZ, the Firebirds started laying down heavy fire into the trees located below our approach path. I told my gunners to go hot as we began our descent. There were tracers flying in all directions. The Firebirds were flying right alongside us, firing their rockets and miniguns. The noise was deafening as the guns opened fire. I glanced over at this poor new guy and watched as he slowly sunk lower and lower into his seat, a look of sheer panic on his young face. I keyed my intercom and told him not to worry, that the tracers were ours. Of course, as I told him that, I knew better, I could see the tracers coming up from the ground through the chin bubble. They looked like they were coming right between our legs.

We continued our descent, and I was at the point of setting the Huey down, when I caught a glimpse, out of the corner of my eye, of my copilot's arm and hand moving. He was waving his arm, pointing frantically. I looked out and saw a line of machine gun bullets hitting the dirt right in front us, and they were coming right towards us. It was just like in the movies. I immediately pulled pitch and got the hell out of there. Why my copilot did not use the intercom to warn me, I'll never know. I believe he was scared speechless.

That was the way the flying was going. Every day we were taking fire as we tried to resupply the ARVN troops. One day I was flying with Lt. Don Wolcott. He had already been promoted to aircraft commander, but because we had run out of copilots, they paired Wolcott, who was a new AC, with me, the SAC. (After the war I learned why we were so short of pilots—the 71st AHC was about to stand down before Lam Son 719 came up. If Lam Son 719 had not had happened, a lot of us would have gotten to go home in January. So much for my luck.) Anyway, Lt. Wolcott and I were trying to get into one of the many LZs. The unit in this LZ had declared a tactical emergency, and our mission was to get supplies in and extract some wounded soldiers. Wolcott was flying, with Trull as our crew chief and Callahan as our gunner. I could not ask for a better crew. We made it safely into the LZ without taking any hits. Wolcott set the aircraft down and my crew started to throw the supplies off. We had been in the LZ for a few seconds when we heard a loud explosion. A mortar landed about thirty yards behind us. Wolcott immediately picked the aircraft up to a hover and nosed the cyclic forward to depart. I saw the ground pounders, through our windshield, running towards us with stretchers. I put my hand in front of the cyclic and stopped the forward movement of the chopper.

I figured since we were already there, that we should at least take some of these wounded guys out with us. The troops nearly reached the aircraft with their stretchers when another mortar landed a few yards in front of us. Wolcott shoved the cyclic forward and off we departed. This time, I did not stop him. We were not more than a hundred feet or so out of the LZ when a third mortar hit. This one landed right in the center of the LZ where we had been hovering. Then to top it off, Callahan came over the intercom and reported that the people on the stretchers were in body bags. We had been briefed that they were wounded soldiers, not dead soldiers. I was quite glad that I did not stop Wolcott from leaving the second time—a few seconds later and we would have been blown to hell and back.

Since this was such a big operation, there was a lot of press out at Khe Sanh trying to get shots of the action. One day our assignment was to fly some reporters and photographers out along the Laotian border and let them shoot some moving pictures of the action in the area. I was told under no circumstances was I to take these reporters across the Vietnam border into Laos.

Personally, I did not like flying reporters—I had seen firsthand the effect the press had on the war effort. I thought they were doing more harm to the war effort than any other single group. But I had a job to do, so I brushed my personal feelings aside. We had been briefed to pick up the reporters at Khe Sanh airstrip, take them up for a few hours of filming, and then return them safely back to Khe Sanh. We set our chopper down at one of the landing pads at Khe Sanh, and the reporters came over and introduced themselves to us. Right away, they began asking my crew if they had pictures of the war. They even offered my crew money for pictures of Soviet tanks. Of course, my crew did not have any.

We took off and headed southwest from Khe Sanh, down Route 9 towards where all the action was taking place that day. There was a lot of action going on, and the reporters had their cameras clicking away. I followed the action up one of the rivers. We spotted a team of F-4 fighters working out along the river, and they started to film them doing their bombing runs. As we were circling watching all this action, the reporters kept begging me to fly over into Laos. They wanted to be the first to shoot footage in Laos. I kept telling them I could not do that. We were flying along a river that I thought was the border between Laos and Vietnam when I realized that I had made a mistake. I had followed the wrong river, and we were actually filming in Laos! Luckily for me, the reporters were unaware of my error, and once I realized this, I quickly headed back into Vietnam. I thought this was a great joke on the reporters, giving them the footage they wanted in Laos without them knowing it.

While we were flying out in the field, we always monitored Guard frequency (243.0 UHF) on the radio. This way, if someone put out a Mayday call, we would hear it and be able to respond if it was in our local area. The air force would also broadcast the B-52 bombing drops on the Guard frequency. Every time we heard a TPQ Alert (time position quadrants), we would check the grid quadrants to make sure that we were not flying in the area where they were going to drop their load. The TPQ Alert would sound something like this: "Attention all aircraft on Guard, this is a TPQ Alert. Stay clear of XD 7538 (the reference was to the map grid) from 31 to surface for the next 15 minutes, Underdog out."

While we were up at Quang Tri, and especially when we were out around Khe Sanh, we noticed the Guard frequency was very busy. Most of the helicopters getting shot down would be working a company-assigned frequency for that day and would broadcast their Mayday call on that frequency. Most of the calls on Guard that we heard were from air force or navy pilots. Several times, we heard pilots being shot down, and I would immediately get out our map, check the grid coordinates, and see if we were within range to pull a rescue. Most of the time, the pilots were over in North Vietnam. Usually an Air Force Jolly Green Giant rescue pilot would answer the distress call. If no one did, then we would answer and relay the message to the proper rescue unit, since we were not allowed to go into North Vietnam.

The air force used the Sikorsky-built helicopter, the S-65/HH-53, for their rescue chopper. This helicopter was the largest built in the free world. It could attain a top speed of 189 mph, which was considerably faster than the Huey.[22] The air force would take these huge helicopters and fly them into North Vietnam to rescue the downed pilots. I really had respect for these rescue pilots. There was a standing joke that in order to qualify to fly one of these aircraft, you had to pass a special test. All the pilots who wanted to try out for the position would line up, and the first thing that you were required to do was to take your balls and be able to throw them over your shoulders, because believe me, they had "Big Balls"!

I was always amazed at the differences in the voices of the individual pilots as they put out their mayday call. A lot of these calls were made after being shot down and ejecting from their aircraft, while they were hanging from a parachute over hostile territory. Some of these pilots' voices were so calm that you would think that this was an everyday occurrence for them. They would put out their "Mayday, Mayday," followed by their grid coordinates in a soft, calm voice. Then there were the screamers. Their voice would send shivers down my spine as I listened to them. You could tell that they were in sheer panic as they blurted out their radio call. I really felt bad for those guys. But the majority of their voices sounded excited, yet very professional. I always wondered if these downed pilots got picked up or not.

We were flying so much that we were exceeding the monthly 140 hours that the army allowed us to fly. At the point that you hit 140 hours, you had to go see the flight surgeon to get approval to continue to fly. All the flight surgeon did was look into your eyes and ears then ask you how you felt and if you wanted to fly. We would say "sure," and he would approve us for the following day. This checkout by the flight surgeon became a nightly event.

CHAPTER 12

LZ LOLO

February was going by fast. Lam Son 719 had turned into a full-fledged war. The ARVN units we were supporting were meeting heavy resistance everywhere. Up at Ranger North, the 39th ARVN Rangers had to fight their way over to Ranger South, leaving over a hundred dead behind and several wounded.[23] The ARVN forces at LZ 31 got overrun.[24] They were taking heavy casualties, along with the American aviation units that were supporting them. There was no safe haven for helicopters; they were getting shot down everywhere.

Even the gunships were taking heavy losses. It was standard operating procedure (SOP) for our gunships to work in teams of two. Because they worked in teams, the NVA figured out they could set up a trap by putting three of their .51 cal. machine guns in a triangle. When the gunships made their gun run on one of the spotted .51 cal. positions, the other two machine guns would wait until the second ship had finished its gun run and was pulling up and away. Then they would open fire. It was a great tactical ambush—we heard that several Cobras had been shot down this way. This triangle ambush was working so well for the NVA that some of the aviation units were banning the Cobras from attacking .51 cal. positions. Later on, when the ground units came upon some of the .51 cal. positions that had been blown away, they discovered that the NVA had been chaining their gunners to the guns so that they could not run, forcing them to stay and fire. Incredible!

Back in our company, Fast Teddy was still pulling the same old crap. When Major Davis had been our CO, he handled our pilots with respect and received respect in return. The senior aircraft commanders had always run our flights and missions because they had the most experience and knowledge. You became a SAC by experience and leadership, not rank. But when Fast Teddy came in as our new CO, he decided to disregard this. He wanted commissioned officers to run the missions and be flight leads. The warrants had nothing against commissioned officers—we had several that were excellent pilots and leaders. The problem lay in the fact that most of the SACs at that time were warrant officers. That was where the experience was. Now, because of Fast Teddy's order, we would have the inexperienced leading the experienced. This did not seem logical to us, but for Teddy, we were to find out that this was him at his best. Logic meant nothing and personal emotion meant everything.

Overnight the junior ACs, because they were commissioned officers, were leading the flights, with the SACs in the rear of the formation. They would be trying to run the flight on the UHF radio, while on the VHF radio the SACs would be telling them how to do it. I knew and understood that it was just as hard for these poor junior ACs being forced into running the flights as it was for the SACs being forced out.

The night of March 2 a group of us were sitting around talking about Fast Teddy and how disgusted we were with him. We could see how demoralized our men were becoming and could not believe that one man could make such a difference in our company's morale. After much debate, we decided that we had had enough of Fast Teddy and needed a break. Several of us, including myself, decided that we would take tomorrow off and not fly. We were worn out from flying more than 140 hours per month, so all we had to do to ground ourselves was tell the flight surgeon that we were fatigued and did not feel safe to fly. In this way, several of us from First Platoon grounded ourselves via the flight surgeon. There would be no flying for us tomorrow.

March 3 was supposed to be a typical day of flying. Our unit would be participating with other aviation units to insert a battalion of 1st Infantry ARVN troops into an LZ, over in Laos, called Lolo. Their mission was to establish a fire-support base. Unknown to us at the time, LZ Lolo was going to be one of the worst helicopter disasters of the Vietnam War.[25]

By the afternoon of March 3, we ended up losing two helicopters from the 71st, aircraft #269 and aircraft #358. Both were total losses and were never recovered. Aircraft #426 and #383 were shot up extensively.[26] A Company 101 Assault Helicopter Battalion (AHB) ended up losing two aircraft and B Company 158 AHB ended up losing an aircraft. Our sister company, the 174th AHC, ended up losing two gunships during action near Lolo. Total losses to all aviation units involved added up to eleven Hueys shot down and over thirty more receiving combat damage. This was one of the darkest days in the Vietnam War's aviation history.[27]

Since I was not flying that day, I cannot account for exactly what happened during that insertion at LZ Lolo, but I can relate what I was told by the men who were flying that day. The briefing took place at Khe Sanh. Lolo was a single-ship LZ, so the flight would be in a trail formation led by the Rattlers. They had been told that the LZ was secure; therefore there would be no gunships for cover. They would load troops at a pickup zone (PZ) and then proceed to Lolo, the drop-off zone.

Captain Dan Grigsby flew Chalk One, the first ship in the formation. His copilot was not from our company, due to our pilot shortage. Chalk One started taking fire on short final but was able to land in the LZ and drop off the troops. Grigsby's bird made it out of the LZ but ended up taking hits and had to return to Khe Sanh. WO Gary Arne flew Chalk Two and was from second platoon. He was flying aircraft #269 with Captain Carl Brugger, who normally worked in maintenance, as his copilot. They also started taking intensive fire while on short final, receiving hits in their windshield and tail rotor. They lost their hydraulics, and to make matters worse, their transmission seized and they crashed. In Arne's own words:

> During the briefing the night before at Khe Sanh, I remember this colonel telling us that this was a secure LZ, a piece-of-cake mission. We were also told there would be no gun cover for the insertion because it was a secure LZ. Several crews even talked about not wearing chicken boards. We hadn't flown in Laos before, so we didn't know any better. I decided that we would wear our plates and be prepared for the worst! I'm alive today because of the chicken plate.
>
> We picked up the ARVNs in Laos and formed up the flight. We stayed low-level most of the time. I remember making two false inserts. Then we got down to the real thing. I listened to Chalk One

talk with the C&C ship until he finally identified the LZ. With no smoke to identify a secure LZ, I remember thinking, "That briefing was bogus!" I told my copilot to get on the controls with me in case things got bad. I watched Chalk One go in, but didn't see him take any fire. I was twenty to thirty seconds behind him. Just as Chalk One was leaving and starting to talk on the radio, we got real busy.

We were about one hundred feet up when the windshield explodes and I take three rounds in the chicken plate and three more in the sliding armored plate on my seat. They continue to rake the left side of the Huey. The crew chief, Johnny Blackburn, yells that he has been hit. Next the tail rotor gets shot out because we start to spin, not fast but we were spinning. I decided that we'd try to fly back to Khe Sanh rather than attempt to land in the LZ without a tail rotor. So I set up to keep flying rather than touch down. Just as we pass over the LZ, the hydraulics go out. I was glad that the copilot was on the controls with me. We picked up a little airspeed, maybe forty knots and the tail was starting to streamline some when the engine quits. With only jungle to the front, we give it hard left cyclic to try to get back near the LZ. We were coming in about 45 degrees to the LZ and were getting low, maybe ten feet or so, when the transmission seized. We fell the rest of the way and the ship crashed on my side.

The copilot and I climbed out through the back. I expected to see a few ARVNs in the ship someplace but there were none and that surprised me. The gunner joined us behind a log. We counted noses, then I went back and got the crew chief. We dressed his leg wound. He had been hit below the left knee. We could see NVA running off the LZ in all directions. We couldn't see any ARVN but we were some distance from where they were going in. We only had one weapon, the .38 the copilot was carrying. I left the shotgun I carried in the ship. Not long after that, an NVA started running from the LZ and literally jumped over our log. He had an AK and the copilot started shooting at him with the .38. I grabbed his arm and said, "What are you doing?" "Trying to kill the sucker. Isn't that what we are suppose to do?" he said. I replied, "Don't attract any attention. He has an AK and can kill us all in a minute!"

We stayed behind the log for about an hour, then started to move up towards the LZ. We got part way and stayed behind another log for another hour. The ARVNs threw a lot of grenades as they expanded their perimeter. One went off about ten feet from us but didn't hurt us. After the third hour we saw these Vietnamese waving at us to come up to them. We couldn't tell if they were ARVN or NVA, but we went anyway because we couldn't have gotten away.

I remember there was an American captain using a radio to call in artillery and doing a wonderful job. He knew what he was doing on the ground, but we didn't. He must have been part of the crew of another ship that was shot down. It was unbelievably hot on the ground and we didn't have any water. When I removed my chicken plate, there were three armored bullets sticking through the backside. I was one lucky soul.

There was plenty of war on the LZ. AK and .51 cal. fire went over our heads constantly. The LZ was being mortared. You didn't want to be on the LZ itself, just on the periphery. I watched a Huey come into the LZ on fire. They landed fine and everyone got out but the copilot forgot to duck. He was hit in the head by the blade and died. I had the unpleasant task of retrieving his dog tags. I watched several medivac ships come and go. Finally it was our turn. I helped my crew chief onto the ship and jumped on myself.

WO Doug Womack, who was also from second platoon, flew Chalk Three. He was flying bird #383 with Mike Flatum as his gunner. After Arne went down, Womack made a 360 degree turn to see if the C&C ship was going to abort the mission. They did not, so Womack continued in. Chalk Three did not take any hits on the way in, but once inside the LZ, their bird sustained a lot of damage. Womack said that his ship was rocking in the LZ and he thought that it was the center of gravity changes from the ARVN soldiers jumping off, but it was actually bullets hitting hard points. They took a hit in their skid, one into the frame, and one into the gunner's machine gun mount, which saved his life. A round also passed just to the left of the gunner's head into the transmission. They later found out that the fuel filler cap had shrapnel all around it and that one of the main rotor blades had an

18. Warrant Officer Doug Womack. Doug flew Chalk Three at LZ Lolo. (Photo courtesy of Doug Womack.)

entry and exit hole from the same round two feet apart. Womack made it out of Lolo and milked his ship back to Khe Sanh.

Lt. Kerry McMahon flew Chalk Four in aircraft #358, with a copilot from the Comancheros, due to the pilot shortage, and with Will

Fortenberry as the crew chief. They made it into the LZ but could not make it out. They took several hits, with one hitting the transmission. Lt. McMahon explained to me what he experienced:

> The assault lift required sixty ships. There were not enough lift helos available; therefore two companies from the south sent some of their helos to support the insertion. I had a copilot from a different company. Because so many crews were involved, only the aircraft commanders could attend the briefing. The 71st was assigned as the lead company. We had the first nine aircraft in formation and the 60th aircraft was also a Rattler. In the briefing, we were told that there would be two B-52 strikes on the LZ. We were instructed to keep about one mile in trail of each helo.
>
> Everything went fairly smooth enroute to the LZ for the lift ships. Then things changed drastically going into the LZ. To me, it didn't look like there had been much damage to the area from an air strike. The lead ship landed in the zone and dropped off his troops. He radioed that the zone was hot and that he was taking fire from everywhere. WO Gary Arne was next. He started into the LZ and started taking hits on both sides. He started breaking off and was about 100 feet in the air when he lost control of his tail rotor. I still can see the ARVNs falling out of the aircraft as it was spinning. Arne was still trying to get away from the LZ when they shot out his engine. He tried to autorotate back into the LZ, but didn't make it. I do not remember who Chalk Three was.
>
> As I started into the LZ, we were taking .30 cal. fire from the left side. I think the NVA was using a large dead tree as an aiming stake because several other pilots said they started taking fire right after passing that tree. The rounds started hitting my door and the sliding chicken board. I remember the forward closing rod of the door being bent up to look like a fishhook. Will Fortenberry, our crew chief, later told me that the ARVN sitting behind me was hit and fell out of the aircraft. We were still about fifty feet in the air. The ARVN sitting in front of the gunner was hit and he also fell out. Fortenberry also said that we took several more hits in the tail boom.
>
> I remember starting to bring the aircraft to a hover, when an explosion from behind lifted the ship and threw us into some trees!

> The rotor blades started hitting the trees and it sounded like the transmission was going to be ripped out. I remember shutting everything off, grabbing my hat, and jumping over the center console because my door wasn't going to open. I grabbed a M16 that was on the floor and looked around but didn't see any of my crew. I jumped out on the left side and saw the copilot of one of the lift helos waving me to their aircraft. I saw the rest of my crew on the aircraft so I ran over to the helo and dove in.

Luckily for Chalk Four, Chalk Five came in right behind them and unloaded their troops. McMahon and his crew jumped on board and were lifted out. Chalk Four was the second aircraft to get shot down. At that point, the Chalks started getting mixed up between the Rattlers and the Comancheros. From what I heard, there was a lot of confusion. The Sharks ended up losing two Charlie model gunships. The Comancheros lost two Hueys. Several more ships were shot up. The Lancers also lost a Huey in Lolo to a rocket-propelled grenade (RPG) hit.

My gunner, Pat Callahan, was flying with Fast Teddy that day. As Callahan recalled, "I can't remember exactly what chalk we were that day, but I think around 8 or 9. We had a good view of the first aircraft going into Lolo. We never made it into Lolo ourselves, but had taken a couple hits. When they aborted the first insertion, we returned to Khe Sanh. Kaiser put himself in for a Silver Star and I ended up getting a Distinguished Flying Cross. What for, I sure don't know? We didn't even go into Lolo or do anything special at all!" Lt. McMahon confirmed Fast Teddy's "heroic" event: "They flew us back to Khe Sanh from Lolo. It was there that I saw the Ops O's and the CO's [Kaiser's] helo and heard how they had not even dropped off their troops after taking one small arms hit in the right side of the aircraft."

Back in the company area, we were told what was going on. We were all upset, but not surprised. We were told that Arne and his crew had their tail rotor blown off and were last seen going out of control and crashing into a hillside. His crew was lost. We were also told that McMahon had been shot down in the LZ.

I was upset. Up to this time in my tour, I had been good at containing my emotions and had not allowed them to break through. All of a sudden, I found my eyes tearing up. Up to this point in Lam Son 719, we had not lost any crew members, and now to lose four and possibly more! It really tore me up. The rest of the pilots and I hung around our company area all day waiting for more information on this disaster. From what we were hearing, rather than aborting the mission, the C&C ship kept the insertion going into Lolo throughout the day. After the first assault was blown, they tried a second assault and so on. The word that we kept hearing was that it was utter chaos.

Around 1800 hrs, someone rushed in with word that Arne and his crew had survived the crash. Somehow they had joined up with the ARVN troops on the ground, fought off the NVA, and finally were extracted successfully from Lolo. What a relief! Here we had them dead and almost buried in our minds and now they were back alive. Arne later recalled, "When I got back to camp, they had already rolled up my bedroll and tagged my stuff to be shipped out. The next morning, I went to the hospital and ended up sleeping for three days."

By some miracle, not one soldier from the 71st died that day. The Lancers were not as fortunate. The copilot and crew chief on the fifth bird the NVA shot down in Lolo both died. Their Huey was hit by an RPG and caught fire instantly. As Arne noted in his account earlier, the copilot, Lt. Charles R. Anderson, was hit in the head by the main rotor blade as he exited his aircraft, dying instantly. The crew chief received a head wound and was evacuated out of Lolo but died soon after.[28]

Later that night, our maintenance had to work on nine birds and ended up replacing nineteen rotor blades on Rattler helicopters. WO Paul Flannery, one of our maintenance officers, told me, "We had so many rotor blades to replace that the blades looked like lumber stacked in a pile."

It was obvious that several mistakes were made that day. I asked myself, "Why didn't they prep the LZ before making the insertion instead of doing it the night before? Why didn't they have gunships for cover? Why didn't they abort the mission sooner and call in some B-52 arc lights on the area before continuing the assault? Why, Why, Why?"

CHAPTER 13

LANDING ZONE DELTA

On March 5, one of our Firebird gunships got shot down. WO Wendell Freeman and WO Pat Riley were operating their Charlie model gunship out west near LZ Alouie, supplying gun cover for a downed aircraft. Freeman explained to me, "It was late in the day and I had just told my crew, Dalferro and Betts, to go hot, when we started taking .30 cal. fire. We were flying low-level at about 125 knots, when my feet were suddenly blown off the foot pedals and up into the instrument panel! We took a direct hit in our belly by an RPG. Luckily for us, the RPG failed to explode. When this hit happened, Riley instantly took over the controls of our damaged bird. He immediately jettisoned the rocket pods and flew our damaged gunship down in a semi-controlled crash landing."

Having survived the crash, the crew continued to take intensive fire from the enemy. Crew chief Paul Dalferro and gunner Jimmey Betts diligently stayed at their guns, putting out a heavy barrage of fire at the enemy, but their situation was worsening. WO Hubert Collins and WO Michael Friel were flying as their wingman (gunships always flew in pairs). There were no other aircraft in the vicinity to do the rescue. Normally a slick would be used to pick up a downed crew, but without one being available and time being critical, they would have to rely on their wingman. Collins brought his gunship in under heavy fire, taking several hits as he landed his bird about a hundred yards from the downed gunship.

Freeman's crew initially thought that their rescue ship had been shot down, so while they were fighting off the enemy, Riley dropped down on his belly and started to crawl towards what he thought was a downed ship to give aid. Meanwhile, Tony Catalina, one of the gunners on Collins's ship, grabbed his gun and headed towards Freeman's ship, fighting the gooks as he went while the other gunner stayed at his gun and continued to fire. As Riley crawled closer, he could see Catalina fighting off the enemy and could tell that the rescue ship was still able to fly, so he crawled back to get his crew. Once back at his ship, Riley gathered the crew and they fought their way over to the rescue ship. After everyone climbed aboard, Collins then lifted off and flew his ship out through the heavy fire to safety. Thank goodness Freeman's crew was only down for fifteen to twenty minutes and everyone got out alive.

I went back to flying the next day after Lolo. A few days later, I reported for a briefing. The officer in charge explained that we would be flying resupply into fire-support base Delta. We were told that the situation at Delta was critical—they were completely surrounded by

19. Warrant Officer Pat Riley and Warrant Officer Wendell Freeman sitting on ammunition crates. (Photo courtesy of Wendell Freeman.)

the NVA and had not been resupplied in several days. We were also informed that there was an NVA regiment located in the immediate area around Delta, and odds were that Delta would be overrun. Our mission was to fly supplies of food and ammunition into Delta, along with cargo nets and straps for Chinooks to come later to lift the heavy artillery out before Delta was overrun. Finally, on our way out, we were to haul the wounded. What made this briefing different from the others was how the officer ended it: "We have to get into Delta at whatever the cost!" My first thought was, "If it's going to be that bad and they expect us to have that much trouble getting the slicks in, then how in the heck do they expect to get the Chinooks in to lift out the artillery?"

We had a flight of seven slicks assigned to us for the mission, with the Firebirds for our gunships. I was in charge of running the flight that day and would be flying the C&C ship. I would be carrying a lieutenant colonel in charge of running the mission. I set our flight up in a trail formation and put WO Gary Arne up in high ship, meaning he would circle at altitude as a rescue ship in case one of the other birds got shot down. I figured he would be able to take it easy in the high ship after being shot down at Lolo earlier in the month and spending three days in the hospital. Boy, was I to be mistaken.

That morning the winds were blowing hard and constantly changing direction, which would add to the difficulty of the insertion. I did a high recon of the area and determined what I thought would be the best entry into Delta. We had the Firebirds prep the approach path, hoping to kill any NVA that might be there. I had the formation strung out loosely to give each aircraft enough time to make its approach, unload, load, and then get out. As the Firebirds completed their gun run, Chalk One set up his approach and began descending. The gunners went hot as the Firebirds flew right alongside them, laying down cover. I knew right away, by the number of tracers I could see coming up at Chalk One, that this was going to be a long day. Chalk One made it into the LZ but could not set down due to the massive fire. After taking hits the bird had to depart immediately to survive.

WO Ed Albrick flew Chalk Two (call sign "Rattler 11"), and his turn was next. We could see his gunners go hot as they descended into the LZ. Suddenly, the ground erupted with hundreds of tracers coming towards them. They could not make it into the LZ because of the heavy fire and hits they were taking. Albrick decided to break off the approach and started a left climbing turn. As Chalk Two was breaking off his approach, Chalk Three, flown by WO Roger Theberge ("Rattler 12") and copilot David Avey, began to descend. Just then Chalk Two took several hits and went down. I watched as Albrick set her down on a little sand bar sticking out along the edge of a stream. I immediately radioed to the rest of the flight to abort the insertion and then radioed to Arne in the high ship to get down and cover the downed ship. As I was doing so, I noticed Chalk Three continuing to descend into the LZ. Again I radioed, "Chalk Three, abort your approach, I say again, abort your approach." Unknown to us at the time, Chalk Three had taken a hit to the FM antenna cable, severing it, so Theberge could not hear my transmissions. He made it down into the LZ and was greeted with intensive small arms and mortar fire. Being unable to unload all his supplies, he departed right away. Theberge made it safely out of Delta but had to return his bird to Quang Tri because of damage.

The high ship, flown by Arne ("Rattler 25"), had not seen Albrick go down. Already the Firebirds were laying down cover to protect Albrick and his crew from the enemy. To help Arnie find Albrick's ship, one of the Firebirds marked Albrick's location with smoke and then guided Arne towards it. Arne set up his helicopter on his approach and started down toward the downed aircraft. A pair of Firebirds rolled in alongside Arne with their miniguns blazing. There were so many tracers flying back and forth that I thought Arne was going to get blown to hell. As we circled, watching this rescue, I knew that it was impossible for Arne to make it, but he kept descending into that mayhem. He managed to put his bird down on the sand bar right alongside where the downed helicopter was. Albrick's crew scrambled over to Arne's ship, and seconds later they were lifting off. The enemy fire continued, and we knew that Arne had to be taking hits. As he slowly climbed out, we could see the tracers chasing after him. Finally Arne made it to an altitude safe from small-arms fire. We could not believe our eyes. Arne had accomplished the impossible! I turned to the Marine lieutenant colonel and said, "You have to put Arne in for a medal." Arne headed back to Khe Sanh with the downed crew and I sent the rest of the flight back to Khe Sanh to refuel and standby. When

20. The fastest gun in Vietnam, Warrant Officer Hubert Collins. (Photo courtesy of Wendell Freeman.)

Arne got back to Khe Sanh, he discovered that he had taken a hit in his first stage compressor. It was a miracle that the turbine had kept running as long as it had. His bird was another job for the Snakedoctor.

While I flew back into Khe Sanh to refuel, the lieutenant colonel called in a B-52 "arc light" (code name for the devastating aerial raids of B-52s) to be dropped across the approach path that we had chosen to get into Delta. He told me, "The Marines do not leave their equipment in the field and we will try it again after the arc light." As we refueled, the air force B-52s came over at an altitude of thirty thousand plus feet and dropped their load of conventional bombs along the perimeter of LZ Delta. The countryside shook as the foliage erupted in smoke and flames. After seeing the devastation caused from this bombing, we were certain that no one could possibly live through such an explosion. I set our formation back up in a loose trail and headed back out to Delta.

The fires were still smoldering as we began our second insertion attempt into Delta. To our amazement, the first ship that we sent back into the LZ drew heavy fire. I thought to myself, "How could these dinks have lived through such devastation from the B-52 arc light?" Just the vibration alone should have separated their brains from their skulls. They must have had their eardrums blown out, but they were still fighting. It was just incredible.

My gunner, Pat Callahan, was flying with Fast Teddy and Captain Randall. Here is how he remembered the mission:

> We were flying into Laos. I do not remember which LZ we were going into, but it was hot. As we were about to sit down in the LZ, a .51 cal. slammed into the AC's door, shattering the armor shield to his left. The shrapnel from the armor plate hit Captain Randall in his arm, wounding him. The aircraft shook and we started to drift back and to our left. The aircraft was spinning out of control, as Captain Randall and Captain Kaiser fought for control of the slick. Randall would yell, "I got it," and then Kaiser would scream, "I got it," but no one had control of this Huey! Once out of the LZ, I went hot. I felt that the enemy was close and I was not going to go down without a fight, regardless of what these guys were doing in the cockpit. We barely missed a group of trees as we departed from the LZ. We went down in altitude and then finally leveled off. Mr. Gross flew over to see if I/we were ok. He flew to my side of the slick and I gave him the thumbs up.

When I flew down to check on them, I saw that they were ok, but due to the hit in Captain Randall's door, they would have to return to base.

Later I was to find out that the bird was so torn up from Randall and Kaiser fighting over the controls that Maintenance had to replace the entire drive train, including the engine and transmission. Good old Fast Teddy at his finest!

WO Mike Carlisle ("Rattler 10") was flying #770, with crew chief Will Fortenberry and gunner Dennis Moore. Just before it was time for Carlisle to go into LZ Delta, Wendell Freeman ("Firebird 99"), the fire-team leader for the Firebirds, called Carlisle on the radio, telling him that they had just run out of rockets. They still had ammunition for their miniguns, so he could either wait while they go back to Khe Sanh for more rockets, or go in now with just the miniguns. Carlisle told Freeman that he wanted to do it now, because if he did not go in now, he never would.

Carlisle set up for his approach, told his crew to go hot, and descended. The Firebirds rolled in alongside and slightly below Carlisle to give him cover. By then the wind had shifted and was on their tail, making the approach even harder. They were taking heavy fire as they approached the LZ. Carlisle made it into the LZ and pedal-turned his chopper towards the west, so that he could exit more into the wind. Mike told me later, "As I'm turning the Huey in the hover, three dinks pop up out of a hole right in front of us in the LZ. I know that we're dead, but luckily Moore guns them down first!" Carlisle's bird was taking hits and had to get out of there as fast as possible, so he pulled pitch and departed Delta. Luckily, he made it out but ended up taking a hit in his stabilizer and a hit in one of his rotor blades. He had to return to Khe Sanh and have the Snakedoctor check him out.

I decided that it was time for me to try to make it in. I set up on a long final with the Firebirds laying down cover. I was still totally amazed that there were live dinks below us after the arc light. I told my crew to go hot as we descended into a firefight. By the grace of God we made it into the LZ without taking any hits, but it was apparent that the LZ was too hot to survive. We had to brake away as soon as we got there and left Delta without taking any hits. I called an abort to the insertion and sent everyone back to Khe Sanh to refuel and stand by for further orders.

Back at Khe Sanh, I tried to talk the Marine colonel out of going back into Delta, but he said, "No, we will try again after lunch." At least he had the sense to call for a second arc light to be dropped along the perimeter of Delta. It had not been a good morning for our flight. Albrick's ship was down in the field. Arne's ship was at Khe Sanh with a hole in the compressor. Theberge had returned to Quang Tri with his radios blown out. The Snakedoctor was checking out Captain Randall's bird, Carlisle had two holes in his ship, and the colonel was telling us to keep trying! So what were we to do? We would try again.

As soon as the second arc light was dropped, we cranked up what was left of our flight and headed back out to Delta. I kept thinking to myself how absurd this was. We had already demonstrated to the colonel that we could not get our slicks into the LZ without getting the shit shot out of us. How in the hell did he ever expect the Chinooks to sling-load out the artillery under such fire?

The first ship to go in, on the third insertion attempt, was flown by Captain Don Lynam ("Rattler 16"). Lynam explained what happened:

> I told my crew, it doesn't look good. I knew that it was going to be a hot LZ so I decided to parallel the ridge that led to Delta to take advantage of where the prep had taken place. Then I would make a ninety degree turn into the LZ. On short final, they are shooting the shit out of us as we approached the LZ. I lose my radios. There's NVA all over the LZ shooting at us from point blank range. We're taking hits, when all of a sudden a big hole is blown into my door. Something hits my arm and I reach down and pull out a piece of shrapnel from my arm! I pull pitch and dive over the top of the LZ and head down the backside of the LZ. At this point, I give the controls to my copilot, so that I can check out my arm. I look up and there's one tree in the way and the copilot hits this tree. I take the controls back and head back across the border and set the Huey down alongside a river. Due to the damage to the aircraft, I can't shut down the bird. My crew chief has to disconnect the fuel line so that we can shut down the bird.

After Captain Lyman went down, I decided that I would try again to get into Delta. Two arc lights and we were still taking fire—what more could we do? Now I knew how Davy Crockett must have felt at the Alamo. I radioed for Firebird 99 to give me cover as I started my descent. I slowly lowered the collective as we began our descent into Landing Zone Delta. All hell was breaking loose! The Firebird gunships were laying down cover as they screamed alongside us. Their miniguns were puffing smoke, singing their loud, but familiar sound. Their rockets were screeching as they flew past us. I told my crew to go hot, and my crew chief and gunner unlocked their weapons and opened fire. The noise was deafening—our helicopter felt as if it was coming alive from the shuddering and shaking from her guns. Tracers were flying in all directions. Fear and terror saturated the air.

We continued our descent down into the hell below. My crew chief yelled, "Taking fire at ten o'clock." Then my gunner yelled, "Taking fire at one o'clock, no three o'clock. Hell, it's coming from everywhere." We were now only three hundred yards from the landing zone and just about in, when I heard a loud explosion and felt the bird whine, as a shell slammed through the transmission. The Huey reacted with a violent jolt, and then wham—another shell found its mark. I instantly pushed the cyclic forward and pulled pitch, thinking to myself, "We're out of here!" Fire was coming from everywhere and there was no place to hide. Time slowed to eternity as we climbed out, foot by foot, to distance ourselves from the enemy and madness below. We had taken a direct hit in the transmission, but thank God we were still flying. If I could help it, I knew that we could not set the bird down here because it was too dangerous. I had to make it back closer towards the friendlies. Suddenly my crew chief yelled, "Mr. G., she's leaking bad, it doesn't look good." I took a quick look back over my right shoulder in the direction of the transmission. There was fluid running everywhere. It was time to make a decision.

I called on the radio to abort the mission. At that point, we did not have enough aircraft to continue. My next step was to evaluate the damage to my bird. We had taken several hits but the one into the transmission was my major concern. If the transmission froze up, we were all dead. With the transmission slinging out fluid, we had no choice but to put her down before the fluid was gone. So began the race of loss of altitude versus loss of transmission fluid, and I was determined that we would win.

I set the damaged aircraft down, facing west along the dirt road, Route 9, which ran back towards Quang Tri. This area appeared safe since it was still daylight. I also knew that units supporting Khe Sanh were using this road regularly. As I eased the leaking bird down onto the grassy ground, our high ship swung down and set down right beside us. They had already radioed the company and were told that our battalion would be sending a Chinook helicopter out shortly, to lift my bird back to Quang Tri for repairs. Based on this information and judging that the area seemed secure, I decided to stay with the aircraft and make sure that it got hooked up and sling-loaded back to our company. The rest of my crew went with the high ship. They loaded the M60s into the bird, climbed in, and flew off.

Shortly after the high ship departed, a bird dropped off a "pathfinder" with the slings to haul out my bird. A pathfinder was a soldier whose job was to scout out, then secure and cut out landing zones. A lot of times, these LZs were so tight that they would have to enlarge them by cutting the foliage out by hand, so that the helicopter could fit in. This pathfinder looked to be my age, twenty years old, and sported the most unusual haircut for being in the military. The sides of his head were clean shaven, but running down the center of his head, from his forehead to the back of his neck, was a strip of dark hair about three inches thick. I had seen this haircut, a "mohawk," in the movie, *The Last of the Mohicans,* but never in person. Up to this point in my tour, I had seen a lot of soldiers with beards out in the field, but never a mohawk. I really got a kick out of it. I guess with them being out in the field all the time, they could get away with doing this. I knew we sure could not.

We climbed up on the bird and hooked up the slings to the Huey. This way when the Chinook arrived, all we would have to do was attach the sling to the hook under the Chinook and off it could go. I had gone down around 1400 hrs and was expecting to be picked up within the hour. I knew that they would be here shortly because a Huey was worth too much money to just leave sitting out in an unsecured field. The pathfinder and I sat around BSing about the usual; where you were from, how long to go, how has it been going, and so forth Being in the service, you got good at the art of BSing because it helped to pass the time.

We sighted a Chinook off in the distance headed our way. I thought, "Not bad, I'll be out of here in no time at all." But as the bird got closer, it did not start descending or circling. It just kept flying straight and level and within seconds it was out of sight. This happened several times. We would sight a Chinook and watch as he flew over, never stopping to pick up our bird or us.

About thirty minutes before sunset, an armor unit, which had been situated about a half mile south of our location, cranked up and began moving south in a direction that was headed away from us. I had felt pretty safe up to then, but as I sat and watched the armor unit pull away, I felt as if they were pulling that secure feeling right out of my gut. I thought to myself, "Where is our lift bird?"

It had been forty-five minutes since the last Chinook had flown over and darkness was fast approaching. The only weapon that I carried was a .38 pistol, and the pathfinder had a M16. That was the extent of our firepower. I was beginning to worry. Was it possible that they had forgotten us? That did not happen, you just do not forget about a quarter-million-dollar helicopter. Pilot maybe, but helicopter never! I had always said that if I went down, at least I would have the M60 machine guns from our chopper to help protect us. They had been lifted out with my crew, though, which seemed like the right thing to do at the time. Now, I was wondering.

Just as I lost sight of the sun over the ridgeline, Charlie decided to try to take the chopper. First we heard incoming, a loud squealing whistle, followed by a loud explosion. The mortar landed approximately one hundred yards due west of our location. The pathfinder and I both hit the dirt. As I lifted my head, I could see a firefight taking place just west of our location. There were tracers flying everywhere. Knowing that the third mortar or rocket usually hits the target, I took one final look at the pathfinder and he at me, and then we both split. He had his ideas and I had mine, and evidently they were not the same because we went in different directions.

I headed in the opposite direction from where the attack was coming. I knew that there had been some American troops dug in, in that direction, because I had done a quick recon while setting down the bird. I ran about two hundred yards and jumped into one of their foxholes, which was inhabited by two young soldiers—and I mean young! I was only twenty years old myself, but these two boys looked like they could still be in high school. They both gave me this look like, "What do we do now?" My first question to them was, "How long have you guys been in country?" They replied, "About two weeks." I was really beginning to realize that this just was not my day. I told them, "I don't know about you guys, but I'm not going to stay here. I'm going to head south towards where the armor unit has gone and try to join up with them." With only a .38 pistol, I was in no position to make a stand.

I took one quick look to make sure it was clear and then jumped up out of the foxhole. I ran south as fast as my legs could move me. As I ran, my heart and mind were both racing. What had happened to that Chinook? I could have gone with the high ship, but no, I had to stay with the chopper. It sure did not seem like a good idea now.

My instincts were right. I had run maybe three-quarters of a mile when in the dusk I saw what appeared to be an American jeep coming down the dirt trail. They had spotted me and had come to the rescue. They immediately threw me an M16 and yelled for me to hop in. Once I jumped in, they whirled the jeep around and off we went, headed back into the jungle toward their campsite. What a relief!

Being a warrant officer, I was the highest-ranking soldier at their campsite. I explained to them what had happened as far as I knew. The platoon leader told me that they would get on the radio. They would try to relay the message to our brigade headquarters to pass the word down, that I was safe with them.

These ground soldiers really loved the helicopter and its pilots. I could tell this immediately by the way they were treating me. One of the first things they did was give me a Coke, which out in the field was hard to come by. Then they rounded up some C-rations for dinner and even found me a sleeping bag. They were treating me like a king. They told me how they really respected the chopper pilots, because the choppers were always bringing them supplies or extracting them from hairy situations. I sat there eating C-rations and listened to these guys telling me story after story about how this and that helicopter had saved their lives. It made me realize how much the ground troops really appreciated us. I had never really had a chance like this, to just sit and talk with the guys that we flew day in and day out. As we sat there swapping war stories, I suddenly realized that I was actually enjoying myself. An odd thought for being left out in the field. It was funny how a few good men and their appreciation for what I had been

21. Captain Don "Fat Rat" Lynam. (Photo courtesy of Don Lynam.)

doing could make me feel so good and proud. It was a special moment in my tour.

I looked at my watch and it had already passed 2300 hrs. They still had received no word about my company sending a bird to pick me up. I decided to try to catch some sleep. I had barely closed my eyes when one of the guys came over and told me that I better get up. They had just received a radio call informing them that my unit was sending in a helicopter to extract me. I said my thanks and goodbyes to the guys, hopped into their jeep, and was taken to an open field that we would use as the pickup zone.

At first the sound was faint and distant, and then it grew louder as the bird got closer. Whop! Whop! Whop! Whop! The sound of Huey blades beating through the air was music to my ears. One of the soldiers ran out into the middle of the LZ and turned on a handheld strobe light. It was so dark that all we could make out was the pounding of the chopper blades through the air, since the chopper was flying blacked-out. On short final the pilot switched on his landing light and brought the bird to a hover, then lowered her down. I ran over and threw one leg on the skid and hopped in before he had the aircraft on the ground. Before I was even seated, we lifted off into the darkness.

Captain Don Lynam ("Rattler 16"), was the aircraft commander. Lynam was a big guy in stature, an Ernest Borgnine type, with a nickname of "Fat Rat." He was one of the guys that volunteered to come and get me. After he gained some altitude and headed back towards Quang Tri, Don turned his head and yelled, "You're not going to believe this Chuck, but they forgot about you!"

Every evening, while we were up at Quang Tri, we would have a short briefing on our next day's missions. We would be told who we would be flying with and with which unit that we would be flying. They always started this briefing by doing a roll call. It was not until they called my name and I did not answer that they realized that I was missing. It was only at that point that someone remembered that I had gone down earlier in the day. Hearing this made me furious. They had forgotten! I could not believe it. I could have been killed because someone had not done his job. To make matters worse, when we arrived back at our company area, Fast Teddy had the gall to meet me, throw his arm around my shoulder, and say, "We were doing everything in our power to get you out of there." I knew that he was lying, but what could you say to a CO like ours? I chose to say nothing and walked off. I was scheduled to fly the following morning and needed to get some sleep.

Unfortunately, LZ Delta was overrun during the night. The next morning we were given orders for the same mission as yesterday. When we found out that Delta was overrun, I was glad. I felt bad for the ARVN guys, but I was so glad that we were not going to have to do the same flying as yesterday. I knew that you could only survive so many days like yesterday. (Arne ended up being put in for a Silver Star.)

As far as the bird that I was flying yesterday was concerned, it spent the night out in the field by itself. It was in such bad shape that it was assigned to the general support (GS) people. They hooked the bird out of the field and it was sent back to Da Nang, never for us to see again.

22. A Chinook helicopter sling-loading a Huey back to base for maintenance repair. Notice the other Huey down along the trail. (Photo courtesy of Wendell Freeman and Terry Wasson.)

Lam Son 719 was two months of utter chaos for the units involved. We flew eight to ten hours a day, with intensive action taking place hourly. Because of the magnitude of these missions, it was next to impossible to tell exactly what occurred during each one, much less each day. As I mentioned earlier, you could take four crew members from the same aircraft and ask each one of them what happened right after the mission, and you would get four different stories. As the years pass, each person's memory starts running events together. I have gone to great length to contact the people who were flying that day at LZ Delta. Some people chose not to respond to my inquiries. I apologize if I left someone out who felt that they should have been mentioned. I am not saying that the events at LZ Delta took place in exactly the way that I describe them here, only that this is the way that I remember them happening at the time. I personally feel that everyone who flew in our flight that day was a hero in my book.

CHAPTER 14

REALIZATION

March 9th, 1971

Dear Mother,

Hello and I'm fine believe it or not. Been flying so much lately. We just don't have enough pilots. I guess you've been reading about the war. It's really bad. Everyone is getting shot down or shot up. I just wish that they would of waited till June to start this operation.

I don't want you to start worrying, because I'm ok and if anything ever did happen, it wouldn't help by worrying. I have over 1200 combat hours now. Sure could use a vacation. By the time that you receive this, I will have less than two months left.

I've been getting the letters real good and I really appreciate them all, it's just that we are so tired and pushed; it's hard to get off a letter. I hope you understand. It's really hard to believe that I will actually be leaving this place. All I can say is that it's been a long year—soooo-long. I feel that I say the same thing every time that I try to write, but it's really hard to find something to write about.

I found it hard to understand how they could have forgotten about my helicopter and me, sitting out in the field, but they had. I decided that I would forget about building all those flight hours, and so I put in for my R&R (Rest and Relaxation). I had not planned on taking one, but after LZ Delta it seemed like a good idea to get away from Nam

23. Pat Callahan sitting in front of a first platoon hootch. You could not have asked for a better gunner than Callahan. (Photo courtesy of Pat Callahan.)

for a while. All that action was getting too hairy for my blood. The next day I went up to the orderly room and put in for my R&R. The company clerk told me that it would take about a month to get my orders. Oh well, a month was better than nothing.

Several times when we were out flying in the field, my crew chief, gunner, and I would sing our favorite song from *Hee Haw*: "Oh where, oh where are you tonight? Why did you leave me here all alone? I searched the world over and thought I found true luv, you met another an TH—th you were gone." We felt this song summed up our feelings about life. Other times when I started our descent into an LZ during a combat assault, I would hear Callahan come over the intercom and start singing the song, "Please Mister Custer, I don't want to go, forward ho."

The first platoon had a lot of good crew chiefs and gunners. The pilots would spend a great deal of time with their crew. My gunner, Callahan, was always talking about how he was going to buy this new Yamaha motorcycle when he got back to the states. He carried his dream picture of that motorcycle cut out from one of the cycle magazines. It was a green Yamaha 650 Special. He never did buy one when he returned home, but I had heard so much talk about how great a bike it was, that when I got home, I went out and bought one.

I heard that Vietnam caused more "Dear John" letters than any other war in our history. I felt that these Dear John letters gave us a good indication of how our society and its attitude toward sex, loyalty, and devotion were changing. We had a lieutenant in our platoon that was in his early twenties. He was an easygoing, nice type of guy, who was always talking about his wife. One day he received a letter from her, and it was not the type of letter that he wanted to receive. Overnight we noticed the effect that her letter had on him. There was nothing worse than getting a Dear John letter from your wife or girlfriend and not being able to go home to try to resolve (or dissolve) your relationship. I really felt sorry for those guys. As for this lieutenant, he suddenly turned very inward and started volunteering for every dangerous mission that came along. It looked to me like he was trying to get himself killed in combat. I thought that was really sad.

One morning, I flew a major up to Khe Sanh for a briefing. Upon reaching Khe Sanh, I set our bird down in line with six other birds that were parked in a parking area. I parked the helicopter facing west into the wind. The major told us that he would be back in about sixty minutes, so we went ahead and shut down the bird and tied down her blades. A few minutes after we finished securing the blades, the other helicopter crews cranked up their birds and departed. Later, a flight of Huey slicks flew in and landed in the pad, but because the wind had changed, they parked their birds facing south, which was ninety degrees to the way we were sitting. They went ahead and shut down their birds and left. We were left sitting there facing one direction while all the other birds were facing another direction. No big deal, right?

I was sitting up in the cockpit, trying to catch up on my sleep, when another bird landed. I was half asleep and not paying any attention when this full bird colonel jumped out of his chopper and marched toward our bird. My gunner yelled, "Mr. G. you better wake up, a colonel is coming." The colonel walked directly over to the door of my bird and started chewing me out for being parked the wrong way. I tried to explain to him what had happened, but he was not interested in hearing my story, he just stood there and got madder and madder. He shouted, "Don't you salute a senior officer?" I whipped a quick salute at him, but I could tell this just made him more upset because I did not get out of my seat to salute him. He looked back at Trull, who was sitting in the bird, smoking. We were not supposed to smoke within fifty feet of the aircraft. He asked me, "Do you know that your crew chief is smoking in the bird?" What was I suppose to say? I said, "Yes sir." That answer made him even more upset, so he whipped out a little pad from his pocket and asked me for my name, rank, and unit,

24. Relaxing in the back of a Huey. Crew chief McIntire is to the left, with gunner Callahan reclining in the middle, and with the author to the right. Notice the cigarette in McIntire's left hand. (Photo courtesy of Kerry McMahon.)

jotting it down. He informed me that I would be hearing about this and stormed off. He was a typical asshole colonel. There was a war going on, and he was worried about the way our helicopter was parked. I thought to myself, "What were they going to do, send me to Vietnam?"

We were keeping busy supporting the ARVN troops over in Laos. I was flying a lot of resupply, and we were doing a lot of extractions. One day, we were over in Laos doing an extraction from a hot LZ. Our orders were to extract the ARVN guys from the LZ and relocate them to another drop-off point. The area was extremely hot, which had been the norm since coming north, so we went into the LZ hot, with our guns blazing. As soon as we got our bird into the LZ, we literally were swarmed by panicked ARVN soldiers climbing aboard our bird. There were so many of them on our bird that it was impossible for us to take off, due to the excessive weight. Our bird did not have enough power to lift so heavy a load, and I had trouble maintaining our rotor rpm.

I yelled at our crew, "You got to get some of the dinks off the helicopter. We're too heavy and if you don't, we're going to lose the ship!" I could see the crew trying to get them off, but the dinks were hanging on for dear life. Panic had set in! My crew finally had to throw several guys off our helicopter, but as soon as they were thrown off, they grabbed the skids. Soldiers were hanging on the skids as we were trying to depart the LZ. My crew chief and gunner were back there, banging on the ARVN soldiers with their rifle butts, trying to make them let go. These dinks were really scared. Finally, we got enough of them loose so that we could depart the LZ without our rotor rpm bleeding off and crashing. What a relief. Later that afternoon, I found out from other pilots that all our ships had the same problems. The war was getting out of control.

One night, I was sitting in our hootch when a couple of friends came in with some bottles of Mateus wine. Mateus was a Portuguese wine that was very cheap and popular at the time. I had been given the day off, so I was looking forward to a relaxing evening. I was not a big drinker, but not because of my religion—I just did not care for the taste of beer or hard liquor, and as a teenager I had seen the effects of what liquor had on some people's lives. We sat there talking about the war while we drank, and before I knew it, I had consumed more than I should have. The evening passed quickly and it was around 0200 hours in the morning when Charlie decided to start his nightly attack on our compound. Instead of sending rockets at us, he decided to attack the perimeter. We sat there drinking when we heard the start of the firefight. Suddenly, we realized that WO Irby was duty officer that night. We put what was left of our minds together and decided that we had better go and rescue him. We grabbed our .38s and ran out to the perimeter to save Irby. The only thing was we forgot to get dressed. There we were, a bunch of drunken pilots running out to the perimeter in our underwear. To make matters worse, my gunner was on duty that night and he caught me in the act. What a way to impress your crew. Irby took one look at us and asked, "What the hell are you guys doing?" At that point, we really were not too sure. We had just been trying to save our friend. We sheepishly headed back to our hootch and called it a night. Two hours later a fellow pilot woke me up and told me that the company was short of pilots, and I would have to fly that morning. I looked at my watch and realized that it was already morning, time to get up. I thought, "Great, I had just gotten to bed!"

To add to my good fortune, I was scheduled to fly with a lieutenant who I considered to have a bad attitude. I had flown with him a couple of weeks earlier, and I noticed that he did not do much of a pre or postflight inspection. I called him on it, and he said that he did not care to do them and did not think they were that important. I could not disagree with him more. I told him if he did not want to do the inspections, then that was his choice, but if he flew with me, I would not give him much stick time, and so he might want to request not to fly with me. Evidently he did not care, because he met me at the flight line.

I had a total of about two hours of sleep, and now I found myself strapping my hung-over body into a helicopter. On top of that, I had a copilot to whom I had told earlier that I was not going to let him fly. What a way to start the day. Luckily for me, it was a pretty quiet day. By the end of the day, we had logged over seven hours of flying. I had a severe headache most of the day, and this episode helped to reconfirm my thoughts about drinking.

One afternoon, we were departing from one of the many LZs in Laos. This particular LZ was located along the western border of our area of operations. Suddenly, one of my crew members yelled for us to look down. He had spotted some tanks cruising down the trail. Right away, we noticed that these tanks looked different from our tanks. As we took a closer look, we realized they were Soviet tanks. There were three of them trucking down the dirt trail. I had heard tales about people spotting Soviet armor, but I had not believed them. Now, I was a believer. I heard that these tanks had .51 cal. guns mounted on them, so we exited the area as quickly as possible. I knew that a Huey slick was no match for three tanks with .51 cal. machine guns.

Whenever I had a day down from flying, which was not too often, I would spend time talking to the hootch maids. There was one girl that I got along with pretty well, and I took a special liking to her. We spent a lot of time talking. Her name was Lee Thi Com. In Vietnamese, the family name is placed first, as in Gross Joseph Charles instead of Charles Joseph Gross. So her first name was really Com. I was trying to learn some Vietnamese, and she was helping me. She was seventeen years old and lived in the village of Quang Tri. She was about five foot three with a slender build and black hair. I found her outlook on life so different from ours, plus she was fun to tease and talk to. Of course as soon as you started spending time with the hootch maids, most of the guys thought that your only reason was to get into their pants.

As I got to know Com better, she invited me to her village to see where she lived. I was not too sure about this idea. You never really knew if their families were VC or not. Every so often, we would hear stories about how they would catch one of the hootch maids pacing off measurements to make a map of our compound for Charlie. One afternoon, I decided to ride shotgun in the truck that would take the girls back to their villages when they were through working. I found the drive through the streets of Quang Tri very interesting. I had flown over Quang Tri several times, but had never actually been in the village. It took about forty minutes to drop off all the hootch maids and return to our compound. I was glad that I had gone for the ride. I saw a different side to Quang Tri than what I saw while flying over her.

One of the first things that caught my eye was the presence of Americans living in the village. As far as I could tell, they were not soldiers. I guessed they were ex-GIs who had liked Nam and chosen to stay after their tour was over. I had always thought that Vietnam was a beautiful country and I sometimes wondered whose lifestyle was better, theirs or ours? The Vietnamese did not have all the pressures that we had back in the states. Also, I liked how they placed so much value on their families. I guessed these American guys decided to find out the answers to those questions themselves. It was really too bad that the war was taking place. It had really messed up this beautiful country and its people. I had always tried to talk to the Vietnamese, to see how they felt about the war. I was interested in finding out if they had really wanted us over there or not. I wondered if the Vietnamese really told you what they thought or just what they thought you wanted to hear.

One morning, we were low-leveling back to Quang Tri from Khe Sanh, with a load of ARVN soldiers in back. We were a little southeast of Cam Lo, flying at an altitude of about fifteen feet above the deck. I was on the controls when all of a sudden our rpm took off and started winding its way up. We heard a high-pitched spooling sound as if we were having a high-side governor failure. (The Huey has an automatic governor to help keep the rotor rpm constant—it could fail to the high side causing the rotor to overspeed.) If you had a high-side governor failure, you immediately had to pull pitch to load up the rotor and crank your throttle down to reduce the rpm. If you did not get the throttle under control, you could end up tearing the transmission apart and possibly spin the rotor right off the Huey. My copilot grabbed the controls, and then he froze. I could not pull the collective up to reduce pitch or roll down the throttle because he was frozen on the controls. I grabbed the cyclic with my left hand, reached over with my right hand, and slapped him on his helmet to get him to release the controls. Then I grabbed the cyclic with my right hand and grabbed the throttle with my left hand simultaneously pulling pitch and reducing the throttle. By the time I got the throttle under control, I was not sure how much damage had been done to the transmission. The rpm had definitely exceeded the red line.

I brought the Huey down to a three-foot hover and one of our other slicks flew over to cover us. I tried to figure out what exactly had happened. We discovered that by some freak accident, something had gotten hooked on our governor switch and had pulled the switch to max rpm. Next, we had to determine if it was safe to fly back to Quang Tri. I did not want to set the bird down, especially out in the middle of nowhere, but I did not want to lose the rotor either. We sat there hovering in the open field, while one of the other crews relayed a radio message back to maintenance with the details of what had happened and by how much rpm we had exceeded the limit. It took about ten minutes before we received an answer: go ahead and fly the bird back to Quang Tri. Believe me, we babied that bird all the way back to Quang Tri. When we arrived back at the flight line, maintenance pulled the transmission chip detector, and it was full of shavings—time for a new transmission.

On March 24, Rattler Eleven, Ed Albrick, got shot down again. He had been with us a few days earlier at LZ Delta and had gotten shot down there also. That made it twice within a few days. We started calling him "Crash Eddy." They had been doing the usual combat extraction, entering the LZ under intensive fire, when Albrick's bird took so many hits that eyewitnesses said it looked like he was literally shot down in flames. Luckily, he kept control of the aircraft and did a great job of setting the Huey down. The crew got out without any casualties. What luck our guys had!

Lam Son 719 was coming to a close. As soon as the ARVN forces reached their objective, the village of Techepone, they proceeded to occupy it, but then almost immediately decided to withdraw. The manner in which the withdrawal was carried out was humiliating to the troops, and morale in the ARVN suffered. The ARVN had extended itself deep into enemy territory and then had to try to execute an orderly withdrawal while in close contact with the enemy. That was a hard thing to accomplish, and it went bad for the ARVN. The withdrawal turned into a retreat, and in some cases into a rout.

It is easy to understand why this occurred when you look at how the campaign began versus when it was ending. When Lam Son 719 began on February 8, the ARVN had 17,000 troops going up against 22,000 enemy troops.[29] By March 23, the enemy forces had grown to a modern conventional force of more than 40,000 men, including four infantry divisions, a regiment of tanks, several battalions of light and medium artillery, and a substantial antiaircraft capability, all of which pursued a demoralized South Vietnamese Army.[30]

Had it been a success? Not for the U.S. aviation units involved. The army had 107 helicopters destroyed and suffered combat damage to 618, many so badly that they were scrapped. The Americans had 219 KIA, 1,149 WIA, and 38 MIA for a total of 1,406 casualties. The ARVN sustained 7,637 casualties, which included 1,529 KIA, 5,483 WIA, and 625 MIA. MACV claimed 19,360 enemy killed and 57 captured.[31]

Both sides ended up claiming victory. The South Vietnamese had interrupted the flow of supplies and troops down the Ho Chi Minh Trail, and partly because of this campaign it would take more than a year for the North Vietnamese to mount any major offense in the south. They may have met their objective, but the ARVN was now a whipped and demoralized army, with sagging morale due to the high casualty rate. Add to that the fact that many of the wounded and killed were left behind on the battlefield, causing the soldiers and their families much grief.

The way Lam Son 719 was fought by the ARVN showed that the policy of Vietnamization was not working, and that the South Vietnamese were not ready to take over the ground battle on their own. This battle also revealed that the type of warfare that had previously been common in Vietnam was changing, and the ARVN was not prepared for the change. After Lam Son 719, Saigon and MACV had to look more seriously at the possibility of greater conventional warfare taking place in South Vietnam. Within weeks, General Abrams requested an urgent shipment of a battalion of fifty-four M48 tanks to South Vietnam, to thwart the NVA Soviet-supplied armor.[32]

A few days before the close of Lam Son 719, I had been out flying single ship along the Laos border when we looked down and saw the ground underneath us erupting and being blown to shreds. My first thought was that we had flown right through an arc light (a B-52 drop). As we looked closer, we realized this was not an arc light but instead was an intensive NVA mortar attack. I had never seen anything close to this magnitude of a mortar attack before in my tour. The ground was billowing dust and flames. As we watched this mortar attack, I realized, right then and there, that the NVA were going to win this war. I knew that the ARVN did not stand a chance without the help of the United States.

CHAPTER 15

CHU LAI

March 28, 1971

Dear Mother,

Well our operation is over with for our company. We have six flyable aircraft left out of twenty-three which we started with. Everyone's back out of Laos and everybody sure is glad. We're moving back to Chu Lai this week. I guess we'll go back to the same area as before. Everybody is just worn out. Sure will be glad to come home. It's starting to get real hot again. I was hoping it would stay cool until I left. Sure could use a good meal now, our mess is so pathetic. I guess I'll close for now.

The first of April brought a sigh of relief for the 71st AHC. Lam Son 719 had finally ended. In the two-month period from January 30 through March 26, I had flown 285 hours of combat in 56 days. We were worn out and anxious to get back to Chu Lai and our old area of operations. As we packed our belongings, I felt that strange sad feeling come over me again. I was glad that Lam Son 719 was over, yet I knew that I was going to miss Quang Tri. Before I left, Com had given me a golden double-heart necklace. I would end up wearing this necklace for years to come.

Our flight crossed over Da Nang, and as we edged closer to our old AO, I found myself actually looking forward to getting back to Chu Lai. It was a strange thought, since I had never enjoyed Chu Lai when we were there earlier. We moved our company back in on our old flight line, and I moved back into the same hootch I had been living in before we had left for Quang Tri. After settling in, I was pleased to receive orders for the R&R I had put in for up at Quang Tri. I was scheduled to go in the middle of April.

I had been trying hard to reach 1,400 hours of combat flying during my tour. It was a personal goal that I had set for myself back in October. When I had first arrived in country, most slick pilots were flying between 800 and 1,000 hours of combat during their tour. As our company's pilot pool shrank, because of the withdrawal of American support for Vietnam, our guys started flying more than 1,000 hours. Some were leaving with close to 1,200 hours. I had figured if I did not go on R&R or leave, I stood a good chance of breaking 1,400 hours. I had not met anyone who had reached that many hours of combat in a single tour.

I already had more than 1,200 hours of flying, but up at Quang Tri I had decided to forget the hours and get out of Vietnam for a while. I was already in my eleventh month, and I had not been away yet. Most of the guys around my tour cycle had taken their R&R already, plus their leave. (During your Vietnam tour, you were authorized one seven-day R&R and one seven-day leave.) I really wanted to go to Hawaii, but only married soldiers were allowed to go so that they could meet their spouses. Since I was not married, that left me out. My second choice was to go to Hong Kong, but a month earlier the army had decided to stop sending troops there. So I ended up choosing to go to Sydney, Australia. All I had to do was make it through a couple more weeks of flying, and then I would be able to get out of Nam and fly to Sydney for a week.

After our return to Chu Lai, we started right back into our daily routine of flying. We were still putting in some long days. On April 8, I flew 9.4 hours. On the 9th, I flew 9.0 hours; on the 11th, I flew 11 hours; and on the 12th, 8.7 hours. Our missions consisted of flying resupply and combat assaults.

One afternoon we were doing an extraction of ARVN troops. We had pulled the troops from the field and were returning to fire-support base Mary Ann, which was located southwest of Chu Lai. It was situated on a high knoll, just east of a line of mountains that ran from north to south. We had nine ARVN troops on board at the time. I flew over Mary Ann, checked the winds, and set up for a high overhead approach. I crossed over the LZ, lowered the collective, and swung the bird into a steep left descending turn as I had done hundreds of times before. In our descent, as I was turning onto a short final, I noticed out of the corner of my eye that several of the ARVN soldiers had moved forward in the aircraft, so they could see out the windshield. I began my flare, and to my amazement, the cyclic hit the backstops! I had full aft cyclic, which had never happened before in all my flying experiences. The nose was still pitched down and we were screaming toward the ground. Because the ARVN soldiers had moved forward, the weight shift had taken us outside the normal operating envelope of the aircraft, putting our aircraft way out of balance. Being out of balance, we did not have full movement or even normal response of our controls.

My cyclic control was at its rear stop. I yelled through the intercom to my crew, "Get the dinks back where they belong!" We were rushing towards the ground with little control. Because I could not get the nose up as much as I needed, I started sliding below my sight picture, and we were headed for ground contact well below the landing pad. I pulled fifty pounds of torque with the collective, which was the maximum torque that we were authorized to pull without overtorquing and tearing up the transmission. I was counting on the ground effect to help stop our descent (when closer to the ground, airflow through the rotor disc is reduced by surface friction, causing your lift vector to increase with less power needed). I had hoped that getting the ARVN guys to move back would help get the aircraft back into its operating envelope, thus restoring my cyclic control. As I pulled the power in, our rate of descent decreased, and once the bird came into the ground effect, it helped slow the rate of descent. We ended up hitting the dirt about one hundred feet below the pad and bounced off the ground. After the bounce, I managed to get our fully loaded bird stabilized at a hover, one hundred feet below the LZ on a steep incline. Carefully, I hovered the bird up the hillside to the helicopter pad and set her down as the ARVN troops jumped off the chopper. What a ride! Our whole crew definitely knew they were alive because our adrenaline was pumping. What a freaky thing to happen. Thank goodness no one had been injured, and the aircraft had not been damaged.

Back in the company area, Fast Teddy was up to his antics again. The Firebirds had completed their mission and were returning to Chu

25. One of our Firebird gunships. A good picture of what can happen to a bird's skids during a hard landing. (Photo courtesy of Wendell Freeman.)

Lai for the evening. They had been flying low-level when one of their birds had an engine failure. The pilot autorotated the bird down safely and saved his crew's life.

An autorotation is a maneuver that the pilot performs when the engine quits, to allow him to safely land the helicopter. The helicopter transmission is designed so that when you have a complete loss of power the main rotor is allowed to turn freely. You can utilize the air passing from under the rotor through the rotor by lowering the collective pitch lever to maintain rotor rpm. This permits the pilot to maneuver the bird in a steep descent to the ground.

It is very hard to autorotate a helicopter from a few feet off the surface. To execute an autorotation safely you need two things, altitude and forward airspeed. When flying low-level, you have only one of those requirements—airspeed—and not the altitude. So when you are flying low-level and the engine quits, you have to give up some of your airspeed to gain some altitude. Knowing the proper amount of airspeed to sacrifice to gain the right amount of altitude is the tricky part. You throw in the added weight of the rocket pods and it changes the whole equation. At higher altitude, you would jettison the rocket pods to reduce your weight, but if you were low-leveling as the Firebird pilot was doing, you had a split second to do what you had to do before you hit the ground. You definitely did not have time to jettison the rocket pods, and any knowledgeable pilot knew and understood that.

In my opinion, the AC did a great job of autorotating his bird from his low-level position with the time that he had. When he hit the ground, his skids bent upwards from the impact. Upon hearing this, Fast Teddy got all bent out of shape and decided that he would put the AC up on charges for damaging the aircraft. We could not believe it. I felt that they should have given him a medal for saving the lives of his crew, not punish him for the damage that the autorotation caused to his aircraft. You can bet there was a lot of discussion up at company headquarters about this affair. Thank goodness, someone convinced Fast Teddy to drop the charges.

There was always a lot of drinking going on nightly among the officers, and a lot of drugs were being used by the enlisted men. Our company was down to about 65 to 70 percent strength and still flying 100 percent of the missions. This reduction of men but not flight hours put a lot of stress on the crews. Since enlisted men did not have access to the hard liquor like the officers did, they looked for relief from the stress of combat from where they could find it. Where they found it was in drugs. Drugs were easy and inexpensive to come by in Nam. The two most common drugs were marijuana and "smack," a name used for heroin. I was very aware of the drug problem because I was close to several of the enlisted men.

I knew that it was unrealistic to expect all the crew members not to do drugs in the environment within which we were operating. I always told my crews, "I don't care what you do when you are not flying with me, but when you fly with me, you had better be straight." One day, I was flying with a gunner and he showed me a photo of him sitting behind a table, and piled high on the table was a large stash of marijuana. The pile appeared to be approximately two feet wide and one foot high. He was so proud.

One night, around 0130 hours, our platoon leaders came through the company area and roused us from our sleep. We were told that we had to get up and do a drug shakedown of the enlisted men. We were ordered to go down to the enlisted men's hootchs and inspect their personal belongings for any type of drug. It was bad enough that we had to get up in the middle of the night, much less try to bust the guys that we were flying combat with for drug possession. I did not condone the use of drugs, but how could the same officers who were boozing it up nightly go down and bust the enlisted men for using drugs? This seemed so hypocritical to me.

I crawled out of my nice cozy sleeping bag and into my flight suit, and then headed down to the enlisted men's quarters. As soon as I walked into the first platoon's hootch, I heard, "Mr. G., come over here." A couple of the enlisted men called me over to inspect their lockers. They knew that if I found any drugs, I would not report them. So over I went and took a quick look into each of these men's lockers. "Looks okay to me," and I continued on to a few more men's lockers while the other officers did their inspections. I thought to myself, "What a waste of good sleeping time." When everyone finished, we headed back to our hootch to salvage what little time there was left of the night.

April 10, 1971, was one of those days that I will always remember. It was the day before Easter, and we were flying in an area located south of Chu Lai where several Vietnamese villages were located. Many of these villagers were just trying to live their lives and wanted to be left alone. The VC would come into their villages and harass them, and so would the Americans. The army had classified this area as enemy territory. The villagers had been told several weeks earlier to move out of this area because of the VC action in and around the area. They were also warned that if they did not leave this area, they would be considered Viet Cong and treated as such.

That afternoon, we were notified that we would be doing a combat assault into this area. Reconnaissance supposedly had sighted a big force of Viet Cong there. Looking at the sheer number of helicopters and troops in the PZ, I could tell that this was going to be a big assault.

I was flying my bird, #405, and had my regular crew flying with me, with McIntire as my crew chief and Callahan as my gunner. We set our bird down in the pickup zone and loaded up the troops. We were located towards the rear of the assault formation. Once we were loaded, we took off, and our flight formed an echelon right formation as we headed south toward where the assault would take place. It was not until we got close to the LZ that I realized that they were doing a combat assault against these villagers. I realized that some of the villagers were VC, but the whole village? Come on. Just then Chalk One came over the radio and told us to go hot. I was thinking about telling my crew to shoot down at the ground right below us and not at the villagers, when Callahan keyed his mike and said, "I'm not going to shoot at the villagers, I'm just going to shoot at the ground." The so-called enemies were off to Callahan's side of the aircraft. I sure appreciated having men like Callahan on my crew who thought along the same lines as I did. Down we descended into the LZ with our guns firing at the ground directly below us. We dropped off our troops and then departed. I could not believe that they were doing this assault. Even though there were a few VC in the village, most of the villagers just wanted to be left alone to live their lives. I could see and understand how these villagers were trapped between the two opposing forces.

After finishing the combat assault, our flight headed back to Chu Lai. My friend, WO Garrett, was working in operations that day. I had made a special trip into operations earlier in the morning to request not to fly tomorrow, because it was Easter and I wanted to go to Mass. I had not had a chance to go to Mass in a long time. Halfway back to Chu Lai, I received a radio call from operations telling me to report to Hawk Hill to fly the flare mission for the night. I could not believe it. I was already upset about doing the combat assault against the villagers, and then to find out that Garrett had scheduled me to fly flares after I had specifically asked to have the day off? This really made me hot.

I called Garrett on the radio and briefly chewed him out, not giving him a chance to respond. As other birds descended into Chu Lai for the evening, we continued on up the Red Ball to Hawk Hill. When we arrived at Hawk Hill, we hovered over to the POL and refueled. Then I repositioned our bird over to where they parked the flare ship for the night. We shut her down and loaded the flares onto the bird.

26. On our days off there was not much to do but hang around the hootch, play cards, or drink. Photo taken at Chu Lai at the Firebird hootch (from left to right) Pat Riley, Wendell Freeman, the author, and Terry Wasson. (Photo courtesy of Wendell Freeman.)

By then it was getting late and we were hungry, so we went over to the mess hall and got some chow. After chow, we headed back to the bunker that they had set up for the flare crew. It was a dark, old, musty smelling bunker that had a couple of bunks set up and a stack of blankets. We were to hang out there until they called us out for a mission. When flying flares, we never knew when we might be called out. It might be before we went to sleep or it could be anytime in the night or early morning. Sometimes, we would get four or five hours of flight time, and on other nights we might not fly at all.

I usually volunteered to fly flares because I would get to log night-flying time, plus I really enjoyed flying at night. Also, you never knew what to expect when flying flares. One night when I was out flying flares an armor unit that had gotten lost called for help. To add insult to their injury, some of their APCs were stuck in the mud. They called us out to help locate and identify their position. We flew out to their last known location and threw out a flare. The armor unit spotted the light from the flare that we had thrown out and directed us from that location to theirs. Once we located them, we spent the rest of the flight lighting up the sky with our flares. We threw out a flare and then circled until that flare was just about out and then we would throw out another. We repeated this cycle until we were out of flares.

One of the reasons I liked flying at night was because it seemed so peaceful. The one strange thing that I did notice, much different from flying at night in the States, was the lights, or should I say the lack of them. Back in the States when we flew out over the water along the coast line, you could see all the lights inland from the houses, but looking out over the water it would be entirely black, with no lights in sight. In Vietnam at night, it was the opposite. You would see no lights coming from the countryside, but when you looked out over the South China Sea, you would see several. The reason was that a lot of the Vietnamese who lived along the coast were fishermen, and at night they would go out in their boats with their lanterns lit. As we flew, we could see all their boats out in the water. Then when we looked out over the land, where there was very little if any electricity, it would be pitch black. Without any big cities in our area of operations we also did not get the light reflection off the clouds from the city lights, causing the night to seem even darker. The good side was that we got an excellent view of the stars.

After dinner, we hit the sack early in anticipation of flying, but morning came fast without a call to flight. We were still asleep in our bunks when the bright Easter sun spread its shining rays over the horizon. We yanked our tired bodies out of the bunks and headed toward our ship to unload the flares before we could return to Chu Lai. As soon as we finished, we took off homeward bound. When I arrived back at Chu Lai, I found out the real reason why Garrett had scheduled me to fly flares. Our unit was so undermanned that the only way Garrett could have given me the day off was to schedule me to fly flares. He had done me a favor and I had not known it. I felt bad and owed Garrett an apology. I made a mental note that the next time I saw him I would apologize, and then I went to bed.

I had a couple more days of flying and then I was headed off for my R&R. I was really looking forward to getting away from the war. I did not know anything about Australia and was not sure what I would do when I got there. The one thing that I did know was that it would be nice to catch up on my sleep. One of the reasons why I had not put in for an R&R, besides wanting to build flight time, was because I knew that once I left Vietnam, it would be even harder to come back.

CHAPTER 16

R&R

It was finally time to go on my R&R. As I was getting packed, I realized that I did not have any shoes to take with me. One of the lieutenants in our platoon, the one I did not get along with well because of our argument over his minimal postflight inspections, offered to loan me a pair of sandals. I thought his offer was quite unusual, but nice, so I took him up on it.

I had been looking forward to getting away from the war. I caught a military flight from Chu Lai to Da Nang, where my flight to Sydney was scheduled to leave. When I arrived at Da Nang, I ran into WO Buddy Howard, a friend whom I had met the day I left to come to Vietnam. What a pleasant surprise that was, and to top it off, he was going on his R&R and was also headed to Australia. It would be more fun to go with someone, whom I enjoyed being with, rather than by myself as I had expected to do.

I did not know what to expect in Australia. I had never been out of the States before joining the service, other than to cross the Minnesota state line into Canada. Howard and I boarded the charter flight to Australia, courtesy of the U.S. government, and kissed Vietnam goodbye.

We were required to take a quick physical before we were allowed to enter Australia. They mainly checked us for gonorrhea, otherwise known as the "clap." Venereal disease was rampant in Vietnam between all the whores and soldiers. When we arrived in Sydney, we received a list of hotels where we were supposed to stay (even though we were paying for our own food and lodging) and then went on a bus that took us down to those specific hotels. We checked into a hotel on

Bondi Beach, a strip along the ocean with a lot of hotels. I could tell right away that it was a real tourist area.

After we checked into the hotel and took our luggage up to our rooms, Buddy told me that he thought that we should stay there for only the first night. Then the first thing in the morning, we should check out and head out to one of the luxury hotels and get away from all the GIs. Howard was twenty-six-years old and had been around longer than I. It sounded like a good idea to me, so I agreed to do the same. It had been a long flight over and we were tired. We ate some dinner, took a short walk along the beach, and hit the sack early.

The next morning, I woke up and called Buddy. We ate breakfast, checked out of the hotel, and caught a cab over to Kings Cross. The first thing that caught my attention was the speed at which we were driving as we headed towards Kings Cross. It had been eleven months since I had been in a car on city streets, and it really scared me as the cab driver pulled out into traffic and headed down the street. I wondered why I felt like this after flying combat in Vietnam. The cars seemed so close to us and our speed seemed so fast. Our speed was actually a normal driving speed but my senses were telling me different. Within a few minutes, however, I adjusted to the speed, settled down, and got back into the groove of things. My physical reaction to the sensations around me while riding in traffic struck me as being a little odd.

Kings Cross was an area where there were a lot of fine restaurants and nightlife. We asked the cab driver where he thought would be a good place to stay, and he suggested that we try the Chevron Hotel, a newer, high-rise hotel. On his recommendation, we decided to check it out. We were not concerned about the cost of the hotel. Nam did not have a lot of places to spend money and with a wallet full of money, for once in my life, I felt rich. As the cab pulled up in front of the Chevron, Buddy and I took a good look and we decided that it looked like a great place to stay.

We checked into the Chevron Hotel and then went up to our rooms. When I got into the elevator, I noticed a sign advertising that Robert Goulet was appearing in the lounge. I knew then that we had chosen a pretty nice place to stay. We both had gorgeous views of downtown Sydney from our rooms. I was amazed at how beautiful the city of Sydney was as I looked out at her. I had thought that the United States was the nicest place in the world, and I had not expected another country to be so nice, especially after coming out of a third-world country like Vietnam.

Buddy was one step ahead of me. He had already thrown together some ideas about how we could spend the evening. Upon our arrival in Sydney we had received several brochures and pamphlets, which listed tours and excursions that were available in and around Sydney. The city also had a reception center set up for the GIs to help with any questions and problems that might arise. Buddy thought that it would be a good idea for us to take a dinner cruise, so we picked one aboard the yacht *Honey Hush*. The pamphlet advertised a twilight dinner cruise around the Sydney harbor, with a live band playing. The big attraction, the brochure claimed, was there would be lots of single women on board. This sounded like a great idea to me.

Earlier that morning, I thought about calling my old girlfriend. It had been quite a while since I had last heard from her. After a little thought, I decided not to. (Unknown to me at the time, I was to find out later that this had been her wedding day. That would have really been something to have called her and said, "What are you doing?" Then have her say, "Oh nothing, I'm just getting married." I sure was glad I did not make that call!)

Buddy and I headed down to the reception center to sign up for the twilight cruise. One of the requirements was that you had to wear a coat and tie. Luckily, they had a place where you could rent a coat and tie. We went in and got sized for our coats and then headed out to do some shopping. We both needed some shirts, pants, and socks. I also needed to buy some shoes.

If I do say so myself, Buddy and I looked pretty sharp as we walked up the loading ramp onto the yacht. It felt funny wearing a coat and tie as I had not worn one in quite a while. The cruise ended up being everything that the brochure had claimed and then some. In the southern hemisphere it was beginning to turn autumn in Australia, and it was a perfect night for a harbor cruise. The temperature was in the mid-seventies, and the skies were clear.

As we walked aboard the yacht, we could hear the band playing. We scanned the crowd and noticed several beautiful young ladies dressed in party dresses. I immediately started wondering how the cruise company got these girls to come here. They were all so pretty and dressed to the hilt. We introduced ourselves to some of them, and that was one of my first questions. The girls told us that the cruise company advertised that single women between certain ages were invited to come on the cruise at a reduced rate. This way the cruise company would be sure to have ladies on board for the men, plus it was a great deal for the girls. I thought it was a clever idea. It was a lot nicer meeting ordinary girls instead of hookers.

We had a great time on the cruise, and by the end of the evening we had met two really nice girls that we both liked. Their names were Eva and Rita and they were roommates. Since it was Saturday night and they had Sunday off, we made dates for the following day for them to show us around Sydney. To my surprise, the girls lived only a few blocks from the Chevron Hotel. We met the girls around eleven in the morning at their flat and walked down to the Royal Botanic Gardens, located on the waterfront. The Sydney Opera House was at the northwest side of the gardens. Being April in Sydney, it was a beautifully clear autumn day with the temperature in the high seventies. We spent the day getting to know the girls and ate fish and chips in the park. My date's name was Eva. She was my age and did office work for a business in Sydney. She was about five feet four inches high with long blonde hair, brownish green eyes, and a great figure. I could not believe it. I had never expected this to happen. There I was in one of the most beautiful cities in the world with this good-looking girl. The war was far from my mind. What a great day! Later that night when we left the girls at their doorstep, we arranged to have them meet us at the train station after work the following day.

On Monday, Buddy and I boarded a train going west, to where we had hired a guide to take us to the Outback to search for kangaroos. As the train headed west, it made several stops at these little train stations. The further we got away from Sydney, the more quaint the train stations became. Seeing these train stations made me feel as if I were in some type of time warp, going back to the early 1950s. I really liked it.

Our guide met us at the train station with a four-wheel drive vehicle. He was a real personable mate and gave us a great tour of the countryside. I always had thought that kangaroos lived out in the open plains, but to my surprise, they lived in the woods. While we were driving, our guide suddenly stopped the truck and pointed over to a wooded hillside, saying "There's two of them over there." We thought that he was kidding because he had been cutting up with us so much. Buddy and I looked over at the hillside but neither of us could see any kangaroos. Our guide pulled out this big bullhorn and blew it. Sure enough, when he sounded that horn, the kangaroos took off running. He explained to us that this was one of nature's built-in defenses. The kangaroos would sit there motionless amongst the trees and blend right in with the woods. Our guide also prepared us a great lunch. We had what we thought were barbequed steaks, but in fact they were lamb chops. They were good even though I ate little, but Buddy sure enjoyed them. We spent the rest of the day chasing kangaroos, and then we hurried back to Sydney to meet the girls at the train station.

Once back in Sydney, I quickly scanned the train platform for the girls, but they were not in sight. Not seeing them, we walked into a station filled with rush-hour traffic, searching for them in the crowds. As we got closer to the front of the station, we could see the girls waiting by the main entrance. They noticed us about the same time as we saw them. We visited for a few minutes and then decided to go to a show, *Darling Lili,* starring Julie Andrews and Rock Hudson. After the show, we spent the remainder of the evening walking through the Kings Cross area of the city. Eva and I hit it off real well and had a great time, but Buddy and Rita were not getting along, and this would be their last date. By the time we dropped the girls off at their flat, I had already made a date with Eva for the following evening, but it would be a solo rather than a double date. I ended up going out with Eva every night for the remainder of my R&R. I had forgotten how nice it was to be out with a beautiful girl instead of being with a bunch of guys. Eva was different from the girls I had known back in the States. Australian men tended to treat women more like their personal belongings than as an equal, so I think the women were raised to feel a little more subservient toward men in Australia.

We spent a lot of our time together just walking around the streets of Sydney, talking and getting to know each other. I felt as if I was in a dream when I looked at Eva, then thought about the combat flying that I had been doing a few days earlier. Hopefully I would never have to wake up.

I had picked up some dysentery while in Vietnam, and every time I ate I would get the runs. To avoid any embarrassing situations, I made sure not to eat too much during the day or when I went out on dates at night. Since Eva was working during the day, I would normally have her back to her flat around eleven at night. I would wait until I got back to the hotel and then order late room service. The food prices were so inexpensive compared to back in the States that I ordered shrimp or steak every night.

Time flew by as Buddy and I explored Sydney during the day and I went out with Eva at night. Before I knew it, I was kissing Eva goodbye and sitting on an airplane headed back to Vietnam. During those eleven months in Vietnam, I had forgotten how different life really was back home. Now that I had experienced a taste of being out of Vietnam, it would be hard to go back. When I signed back into the company, I started thinking, "Maybe I should try to take my leave." I knew that our company was not authorizing any leaves because of our manpower shortage, but that was not my fault and I should not be penalized for it, I thought. I had become good friends with a clerk up at company headquarters, so I went and asked him, "If I can get authorization for a leave, can you get me orders to go back to Sydney?" He said, "Sure, no problem."

After some careful thought, I went to see the executive officer (XO) and told him that I wanted to take my leave. He told me that our company was not authorizing any leaves. I explained to him that I had been in Vietnam for eleven months without taking an R&R or leave; we were authorized a leave by the Department of the Army; and therefore, I wanted to take mine. To my surprise, he told me that I could take my leave if my platoon leader, Captain Randall, would authorize it. I was not thrilled about having to ask Randall to authorize it. We were not good friends and I had had my argument with him up at Quang Tri. I figured that this would be a good chance for him to get back at me, and unfortunately he knew that I had just gotten back from my R&R as well. But Australia was calling, so I went in and asked Randall for permission to take my leave. He told me, if it were anyone else asking for a leave, he would not authorize it, but he would for me. He said he knew that I had always worked hard and done a good job and to go ahead and take the leave. I was really surprised. Maybe he was not such a bad guy after all. I thanked him and headed back to the orderly room to get my orders cut.

Within two days, I was headed back to Australia. I could not believe it. I had not thought that much about actually going home until then. My DEROS date had always seemed so far away, and I tended to get depressed when I thought about home. Now that I had tasted civilization in Australia, I was anxious to get home.

My second week in Australia was as good as my first. I went back to the Chevron, got a room, and called Eva at work. She was surprised but excited to hear from me again. I arranged to meet her later that night. Life could not be better.

While I was in Australia, I had several older men approach me on the streets. I guess they could tell by my haircut and the way I was dressed that I was an American GI. Most of these men had fought in the war during World War II. They would walk up and just start a conversation. They always wanted to buy you a brew and tell you about their war stories. This made me feel most welcome and I thought it was very nice. Another thing that I really liked were the fashions that the girls were wearing in Sydney. The miniskirt had come in style, and I had never seen anything like it before in my life. I had been fighting in Vietnam for over eleven months and now to see all these girls walking around in miniskirts, wow, what a sight!

On the weekend, Eva and I went to the Sydney Zoo. We saw koalas and kangaroos, which I saw as symbols of Australia, and also an American bison, which Eva saw as a symbol of America. I had to take pictures of both. As we walked around the zoo looking at the different animals, I realized that I was having one of the best times of my life. There I was, halfway around the world, away from home for more than eleven months without phone contact with my family, and yet I was feeling better than I had ever felt. Life is very unpredictable.

Eva had told me earlier during my R&R that she and her girlfriend Rita had been planning a trip to the States that upcoming winter, which would be our summer. I had been excited to hear that and told her that they had to be sure to come to Minneapolis. As our relationship grew it became more important to both of us that we see each other again when my leave was over.

One morning I was walking down one of the streets in Kings Cross when I looked up and saw two of our crew members. It was Will Fortenberry, one of our crew chiefs, along with one of our gunners. I will never forget the sight. Will was dressed in a buckskin outfit with fringe dangling from his sleeves. It was funny to bump into someone you knew so far away from Vietnam.

This leave passed by quicker than my R&R. Before I knew it, I was saying goodbye to Eva again and boarding a plane to take me back to Vietnam. It was hard to say goodbye to Eva—she was one of those special girls that you could spend a lifetime looking to find. As I stood there holding her in my arms, I wondered if I would truly see her again.

Something happened to me this time that had not happened during my R&R. I had totally relaxed, and now that I found myself heading back to Vietnam, I had the shakes. Maybe I had been away too long.

CHAPTER 17

HOMEWARD BOUND

May 5, 1971

Dear Mother,

This will be my last letter sent from Vietnam. I'm down in Saigon, on my way back to Chu Lai from leave. I'll tell you all about it when I get home. I leave Chu Lai on the 10th to go down to Cam Ranh. I should be coming home either the 15th or 16th. Starting to get real excited about getting my tour over with. I'm done flying now or at least I'm supposed to be. So for once I'm pretty sure that I'll make it. I'm really tired and worn out from this past year. I thought it would never end, but I guess even bad things come to an end sooner or later. I guess I won't get much sleep the next week or two. Just be too excited to sleep. I guess I'll close for now.

Love,

Chuck

My flight brought me back into Tan Son Nhut Air Force Base, located in southern Vietnam outside of Saigon. From there, I would have to catch a flight back up to Chu Lai with the air force, on one of their C-130s. The following morning, I checked with the air force on getting a flight up to Chu Lai. They told me to check back the next day because everything was full this day. Since I was not in a hurry to get back to flying, I said sure and took the rest of the day off. I decided to walk over to the Tan Son Nhut Officers Club for lunch. When I walked into the club, I could not believe my eyes. With the classy light fixtures and fancy furniture, it was like walking into an Officers Club back in the States. I was shocked. How could it be so different from up north? The big thing that caught my attention was that the girls working in the club were wearing nylons. I had never seen nylons before on a Vietnamese woman. Unbelievable, this was not the Vietnam that I knew.

I sat down and ordered a sandwich. As I sat there eating my sandwich, I could not help but hear the other pilots telling their war stories. They would go on and on about their adventures, telling all these wild war tales. Then at the end of their tale, you would find out all that really happened to them was that they had taken a hit in their bird. I just had to laugh to myself. It was definitely a different war down south compared to up in Northern I Corps.

The next day, I went back to the flight ops to check for another flight back to Chu Lai, and they told me the same thing, check back tomorrow. I still was not in a big rush, so I did just that. I hung around the barracks catching up on my sleep. I did some reading and watched the movies they showed during the evening.

This cycle went on for a couple more days until I finally caught a C-130 flight up to Chu Lai and returned to our company. By then, I had only a few more days to go before I would be leaving, so I knew I would not have to fly. When I checked back into the orderly room, the clerk told me that I was in deep trouble. They had me listed as being absent without leave (AWOL). It seemed that in my rush to catch my flight, I made the little mistake of forgetting to sign out. When the XO discovered that I had just gotten back from taking an R&R and then had taken a leave, he came unglued. Now with me forgetting to sign out, he had just the excuse he was looking for to get me.

At this point in my tour, I was not too worried. A few weeks earlier, I had found out that the army was offering an option as the men left Vietnam. We were given two choices: either go "indefinite," meaning you were re-upping and would go back stateside for six months and most likely have to return to Vietnam; or be discharged from the army upon arrival back in the States. If you had come into the service with a career in mind as I had done, you would have no choice but to go indefinite. The economy back in the States was bad, so if you had a wife and family to support, it would have been hard to get out without having a job lined up. A lot of the pilots were going indefinite for these reasons, but I would not. I knew that I would never be able to spend twenty years in an organization that was run the way the army was. I decided to take the early out. I was really excited that they gave us this opportunity, but I also felt that the service was taking advantage of the guys that wanted to stay in.

I had less than a week to go, and I had a copy of my leave orders, so I was not too concerned about being AWOL. A few more days in Nam and I would be headed home. Pat Callahan was leaving, so I went down to the flight line to say goodbye. He had been a great gunner and I would miss him. Since I had not taken any photos while I had been in Nam, Pat got us together and took several shots of our aircraft #405 and crew together. When he took the film in to be processed, somehow they screwed up the film while developing it and could not make any prints. So much for our Vietnam photos.

I would not be flying anymore, so it was time to pass on my call sign, "Rattler One-Seven." I had been watching all my copilots closely, looking for the best one to carry on my call sign. I had flown several times with one pilot whom I had really taken a liking to. He appeared to be one of the most natural helicopter pilots that I had ever come across. I knew that he would get voted in as aircraft commander on his first round, so I chose him to take over "Rattler One-Seven." His name was David Avey. (Avey was to be the last "Rattler One-Seven," because in September 1971 the 71st AHC would be deactivated.)

My last two days were spent trying to get all my records squared away. Operations had lost a couple weeks of my flying records, so I would not even have an accurate record of how many hours of combat that I actually flew during my tour. This was typical army; they could not even keep your flight records up to date. I was also told that if I wanted to get my medals, I would have to wait a couple of more days while they squared away my records. I said, "Forget it!" I had always felt that medals were more for the parents of the soldiers that had been killed in combat. The service would award them a medal so that they would not feel that their son had died in vain.

I wanted to keep my flight helmet but they made me turn it in. I really wanted to take my helicopter nose cone home as a keepsake, but

I could not figure out how to get it home. The evening before I was set to leave, I went down to operations to make sure that I had everything taken care of, including all the paper work. The XO was still upset about my leave, and he told me that he was not going to let me leave until I got a haircut. He knew that the following day was a Vietnamese holiday, and because the barber who cut our hair was Vietnamese, his shop would be closed. Even on my last night in country, I had to be harassed. I left ops and headed over to our maintenance facility to say goodbye to WO Flannery. I had really liked Flannery and wanted to make sure that I had a chance to say goodbye to him.

Around 2300 hours, I headed over to the XO's hootch and knocked on his door. When he answered it, I asked him, "Can I talk to you man to man instead of XO to warrant officer?" He said, "Sure, go ahead." So I asked, "Why are you giving me such a hard time?" He replied, "Because you lied to me about your R&R." I defended myself and said, "I did not. I told you that I had been in country eleven months without taking an R&R or leave, and that was a true fact." He came back and said, "You didn't tell me that you had just gotten back from your R&R." So I asked him, "What would you have done if you were in my shoes? I was authorized the leave, and I was only asking for something that the army said I deserved." He thought for a while, and then told me to forget about the haircut. I thanked him and left to go back to my hootch.

One more night, and I would be headed home. It was hard to believe that I was finally getting to go home, for it had been such a long year. The next morning, I gathered my belongings and said my goodbyes to the guys in my hootch that were not flying. After shaking their hands, I picked up my gear and headed down to the orderly room to sign out and catch my flight home. On our flight back we made a refueling stop in Hawaii. I had never been there and was excited to see the islands as we flew in for the landing.

It was late Friday afternoon when I caught my first glance of what I had been waiting so long to see. As our plane descended through the cloud deck, I saw her. There she was, as beautiful as ever, mainland America. We were on final approach to McCord Air Force Base, located outside of Seattle, Washington. It was still hard to believe that I had made it. We deplaned the aircraft and caught a bus over to Fort

Lewis, Washington, where we would be processed out of the army. Because of the late hour, we were assigned a bunk and released for the rest of the day. We were given orders to report the first thing the next morning for out-processing. I immediately phoned my mother to tell her that I was ok, and I was back in the States. I also told her that I would be arriving home the following night. It had been one year since I had last spoken to her. When I got off the phone, I went to bed.

I spent Saturday morning filling out forms and taking my final discharge physical. I was still having bad stomach problems from the dysentery that I had gotten in Vietnam. I was afraid that if I said anything to the doc about it, he might want to keep me around for further testing, so I told him that I was doing great. At 1400 hours on May 15, 1971, I was formally discharged from the United States Army. I immediately caught a cab to the Seattle Airport with a couple of other soldiers. I was finally on my way home.

When we arrived at the Seattle Airport, we ran over to the ticket counter and purchased our tickets for the next flight home. Since we had a few hours to kill, we decided to get something cold to drink. Boy was I shocked, when I was carded trying to go into the bar. Even though I was in uniform, I was told that I was too young to enter. I explained to them that all I wanted to drink was a coke, but they still would not let me in. What an insult! I had just gotten back from fighting a war for my country and they would not even let me enter the bar with the other guys. The ironic thing was, since I had been an officer, I could legally buy liquor whenever I had wanted to in the service. This was my first indication that there were going to be some tough adjustments ahead.

As the plane's tires squealed on contact, I looked out the window at the surroundings. The Minneapolis Airport looked much the same as it had when I had left a year earlier. Spring was in the air and the trees were in full bloom. It had been the longest year of my life and now it was supposed to be the happiest day of my life!

I had torn off our First Platoon patch from my flight jacket because I was afraid that my mother would not understand. The patch was a black spade with skull and crossbones and the caption "1st Platoon Widow Makers." It was a little after 10 p.m. when we landed. My mother and youngest brother Larry greeted me at the terminal. We went down to the lower level, picked up my luggage, and headed home. On the way home, the subject of the war was never brought up. I would find out later that it would not be brought up for years to come. I had just spent one of the most stressful, yet exciting years of my life, and no one except my brother Jim would ask me about it. I believe they did not understand how to react in a given situation, such as when finding out someone is terminally ill and you are not sure what to say to that person, so you end up saying nothing. Perhaps they were afraid they might say something offensive, given that Vietnam was a very controversial war.

When we got home, I made one of my homemade pizzas. That was one of my favorite foods that I had missed and craved while in Vietnam. My high school sweetheart had taught me how to make it, what seemed a lifetime ago. We sat around the kitchen table, ate, and talked about what I had missed the past year I had been gone. Around one in the morning, the Djerfs stopped by to welcome me home. They had been out and had driven by and saw that our lights were still on. The Djerfs had been friends of our family, and when my father passed away, they were there for my mother. I was glad to see them. The next morning I slept late, then went to church. My mother had a date for the afternoon and asked if it was all right if she went. I said, "Sure." I was glad that my mom was finally having a social life. My four brothers were also gone.

I had shipped home a stereo that I had bought through the Post Exchange (PX), and it had arrived a few weeks before my return. After lunch, I carried the stereo into the living room to set it up. As I sat there on the living room floor unpacking the stereo, I suddenly realized how quiet it was. I was home alone, and I had not been totally by myself for quite some time. I then noticed how small the living room appeared. In my mind, I had remembered it being so much larger. As I connected the speakers to the amplifier, I begin to reflect on the events of the last year, the people who had died, the pain, the stress, and the adjustments that I had had to make emotionally. What had it all been for? Was it worth it? Had anyone really cared?

It was late afternoon, and the new turntable was spinning Gordon Lightfoot's "If You Could Read My Mind." As I sat there alone in the darkening light, listening to the music, I suddenly realized that I would never be able to go home, for home was what I had held in my mind for the last three years, but life stops for no one. I looked around the small, empty room, and cried.

EPILOGUE

Vietnam fell to the Communists on April 30, 1975. Of the 58,169 American soldiers killed in Vietnam, 4,906 were helicopter crew members and 2,202 were helicopter pilots. The average age of the 58,169 soldiers killed in Vietnam was 23.11 years old.[33] There were 11,827 helicopters that participated in the Vietnam War, with 7,013 of them being Hueys. A total of 5,086 helicopters were destroyed in the war.[34]

When I look back at Vietnam, I see it through the perspective of a young man eager for excitement but naive about the stark realities of war. The war made me realize that there is a fine line between man and animal, and in war, one has to work hard at not crossing that line. I always felt that we did well as soldiers when we were there, and I was and still am proud of the way our soldiers performed in battle. Vietnam was the first time that the army actually used the helicopter in air assaults, and I am proud to have been a part of that. When I was in Vietnam, I used to talk to the South Vietnamese people, and the ones I spoke with believed in their cause and were glad that we were there. If one takes the time to study the history of Vietnam after the Geneva Accords, they will understand how the country was divided after the defeat of the French in 1954. One will then realize that it was truly a battle between Communists and anti-Communists.

I can still remember hearing on the news about the collapse of South Vietnam in 1975. That was one of those epic events in my life that I will always remember. I realized that all the death, stress, and trauma that our soldiers suffered was for naught. It is hard to come to terms with having left men behind in Southeast Asia and never being able to confirm their death. I think of the parents and families of the

27. The author sitting in the right seat of a Huey when he was twenty years old. (Photo courtesy of Larry Clampitt.)

MIAs and how they never gain closure to their sons' whereabouts. How terrible it must be to live the rest of your life not knowing whatever happened to your loved one. I think about all the young men's lives that were lost. They all had dreams that would never be fulfilled.

What bothers me most is that we could have won the war! It upsets me when I hear people say that we lost the war in Vietnam. That is not a factual statement and it shows that they do not understand the complexity of the Vietnam conflict. Our country was tired of a war gone badly. Our government chose to stop fighting the war and looked for a supposedly honorable way to get our troops out of Vietnam. President Nixon in 1969, with his "Nixon Doctrine," came up with Vietnamization, which was to slowly turn the fighting back over to the South Vietnamese while pulling the American troops out of Vietnam.[35] Our government knew after the large defeat of the ARVN at Lam Son 719 that the concept of Vietnamization was faulty and would not work. They knew that the South Vietnamese Army was no match for the North Vietnamese Army, but they chose to ignore the facts knowing full well what the outcome would be.

I am glad to see that our nation as a whole has learned from the Vietnam experience: not to commit to war unless you are prepared to do everything within your power to win. It is good to see the troops coming back from Iraq hailed as heroes rather than baby killers. Hopefully we will never again do to our soldiers what we as a society did to the Vietnam soldiers.

As for me, when I returned from Vietnam, I spent the next year in emotional unrest. Eva ended up coming to Minneapolis that summer to visit. She stayed for three months and then I sent her home through no fault of her own. The year after Vietnam would end up being emotionally worse for me than the year I spent in Vietnam. I literally went from being a combat pilot in a war zone to becoming a twenty-year-old civilian overnight. I returned to a society far different from the one I had left when I entered the service. While in the military I had been isolated from the free-love hippie culture, the antiwar protesters, and the antiwar sentiment of the press, all of which made it hard for a veteran who was proud of what he had been doing to readjust.

I went back to flight school and obtained my commercial and instrument fixed wing ratings, and then my helicopter and airplane instructor ratings. I worked my way through college by giving flight instruction and by using the GI Bill. Upon completion of school, I flew airmail, air cargo, and corporate. In 1975 I got married to my wife, Pam, and I have two lovely daughters. I always wanted to build a home doing all the labor myself, so in 1980 I took a year off from flying and built a home in Corcoran, a suburb of Minneapolis.

Shortly after returning from Vietnam, I started studying the martial arts. I played Judo during the seventies and in 1983 I started studying the Chinese art of Southern Praying Mantis Kung Fu. In 1987 I put together a women's self defense course and put it on video. I have been teaching martial arts as the head instructor of the Tennessee Southern Praying Mantis Kung Fu Association since 1993. In 1985, American Airlines hired me. I flew Captain on the 767/757 Boeing aircraft, and as of this writing I have decided to take early retirement.

28. The author sitting in the left seat of a Boeing 757 at American Airlines when he was fifty-two years old. (Author's collection.)

People have asked me how the experiences I encountered fighting in Vietnam at such a young age affected my life. As I have looked back over the years on my Vietnam experience, I realize that it has had both negative and positive effects on my life. One of the negative effects since returning from the war is that I have never slept well. The slightest sound or movement will wake me up. This did not fit well with an airline job that required you to spend many nights away from home in hotels. I also had severe dysentery when I left Vietnam. I expected it to clear up shortly after returning home to a normal diet, but it did not. I spent the next twenty years fighting it—it was a curse that was always with me to remind me of Vietnam. Finally, in my early forties, it subsided, and I could eat like a normal individual and not worry about having to find a rest room.

When I see a Huey flying over, I associate it with the vehicle that stole my youth. I feel as if I missed the fun late teens and early twenties that most Americans enjoy. I went from being a nineteen-year-old boy to an adult with none of the fun usually associated with those years. But along with the bad, I have found that there is always good if you look hard enough for it. One of the positive effects that the Vietnam War had on me was in my confidence. Being an aircraft commander, and then becoming a senior aircraft commander at the age of twenty, with all the responsibilities that went with these positions, made me realize that I could accomplish most anything if I put my mind to it. This confidence, combined with the discipline that the army taught me, allowed me after the service to reach for my dream of being an airline pilot. Being a professional pilot is a very skilled and disciplined job. I have used the physical and mental skills that I learned while flying in Vietnam as a good fundamental base to work from over the years. This confidence and discipline has also carried over in my study and training in the martial arts.

Fighting in Vietnam also taught me the value of humanity. It made me realize at a young age how precious and fragile life is. I have come to realize that I would not be the man I am today if I had not flown helicopters in Vietnam.

I will always be proud to say that I was a Vietnam helicopter pilot and my call sign was "Rattler One-Seven."

NOTES

1. "Group 2, Beechcraft 18," *Aircraft of the World: The Complete Guide* (Pittsburgh: IMP, 1997).
2. "Model Super E18S Specifications," Staggerwing.com.
3. "Group 3, Bell UH-1DH Iroquois," *Aircraft of the World.*
4. "Group 3, AH1 HueyCobra (single)," *Aircraft of the World.*
5. Seymour M. Hersh, *Cover-Up* (New York: Random House, 1972), 7.
6. CNN.com, "'Blood and Fire' of My Lai Remembered 30 Years Later," *CNN.com,* March 16, 1998, http://www.cnn.com/WORLD/9803/16/my.lai/.
7. Michael Beaumont, "Bio, Becker James C," P.O.W. Network, 1998, http://www.pownetwork.org/bios/b/b368.htm.
8. Mike Sloniker, "History of Lam Son 719," *Vietnam Helicopter Pilots Association 1994 Membership Directory,* vol. 11 (October 1994): 287.
9. Phillip B. Davidson, *Vietnam at War* (Novato, CA: Presidio, 1988), 641.
10. Davidson, *Vietnam at War,* 637.
11. Spencer C. Tucker, *Vietnam* (Lexington: University Press of Kentucky, 1999), 164.
12. David Fulghum and Terrence Maitland, *South Vietnam on Trial* (Boston: Boston Publishing, 1984), 76.
13. Tucker, *Vietnam,* 164.
14. Fulghum and Maitland, *South Vietnam on Trial,* 85.
15. Henry Kissinger, *Ending the Vietnam War* (New York: Simon & Schuster, 2003), 204.
16. Steve Forrest, "Tet Offensive: A Turning Point in the Vietnam War," *In Defense of Marxism,* http://www.marxist.com/1968/vietnam.html.
17. Douglas E. Pike, *The Viet Cong Strategy of Terror* (Saigon: U.S. Mission Viet-Nam, 1970), 26–30.

18. John Colvin, "The Tet Offensive 1968, General Vo Nguyen Giap," from *Vietnam Experience Nineteen Sixty-Eight,* Boston Publishing, at Vets with a Mission, http://www.vwam.com/vets/tet/tet.html.
19. Ray Stubbe, ed., "A History of the Hill Battles of 1967," *Khe Sanh Veterans Newsletter, Special Issue: 30th Anniversary of the Hill Battles* at Khe Sanh, at Khe Sanh Veterans Home Page, http:/www.geocities.com/Pentagon/ 4867/hillbatt.html.
20. Sloniker, "History of Lam Son 719," 287.
21. Sloniker, "History of Lam Son 719," 289.
22. "Group 3, S-65/CH-53," *Aircraft of the World.*
23. Sloniker, "History of Lam Son 719," 264.
24. Sloniker, "History of Lam Son 719," 267.
25. Jim Fulbrook, "Lam Son 719, Part Three, Reflections and Values," *U.S. Army Aviation Digest* (August 1986): 6.
26. Sloniker, "History of Lam Son 719," 270.
27. Jim Fullbrook, "Lam Son 719, Part Two, the Battle," *U.S. Army Aviation Digest* (July 1986): 41.
28. Vietnam Helicopter Pilots Association, "Cover Photo Analysis E," *Vietnam Helicopter Pilots Association 1994 Membership Directory,* vol. 11 (October 1994), inside front cover.
29. Jeffery Kimball, *Nixon's Vietnam War* (Lawrence: University Press of Kansas, 1998), 245.
30. Davidson, *Vietnam at War,* 649.
31. Tucker, *Vietnam,* 164–65.
32. Fulghum and Maitland, *South Vietnam on Trial,* 96.
33. Vietnam Helicopter Flight Crew Network, "Statistics about the Vietnam War," http://vhfcn.org/stat.html. From Combat Area Casualty File, November 1993, Center for Electronic Records, National Archives, Wash., DC. CACF is the data used for the Vietnam Veterans Memorial.
34. Gary Roush, "Helicopter Losses during the Vietnam War," *The Vietnam Helicopter Pilots Association,* http://www.vhpa.org/heliloss.pdf.
35. President Richard Nixon, "Vietnamization," speech delivered November 3, 1969, archived by the Program in Presidential Rhetoric, Dept. of Communications, Texas A&M University, http://www.tamu.edu/comm/pres/speeches/rmnvietnam.html.

GLOSSARY

Officer Ranks:

General
Colonel
Lieutenant Colonel
Major
Captain
First Lieutenant
Second Lieutenant
Chief Warrant Officer
Warrant Officer

AC	Aircraft commander
AHB	Assault Helicopter Battalion
AHC	Assault Helicopter Company
AIT	Advanced Infantry Training
AMC	Air mission commander
AMOC	Aircraft Maintenance Officers Course
AO	Area of operation
APC	Armored personnel carrier
arc light	B-52 bomb drop
ARVN	Army of the Republic of Vietnam
ash & trash	A term used for carrying re-supplies in the helicopter
AWOL	Absent without leave
brigade	A unit of battalions, also bgd.
battalion	A unit of three or more companies, also Bn.

cal.	Caliber and round of a weapon; .50 cal. is 0.50 inches in diameter
CAB	Combat Aviation Battalion
C&C	Command and control
CCN	Command and Control North
Chalk	Position of an aircraft in a formation, "One" being in first position
Charlie	Nickname for enemy Vietnamese, derived from the phonetic alphabet that pronounced Victor Charlie for the Viet Cong
claymore	A type of antipersonnel land mine
click	A unit of measurement, approximately a kilometer
CO	Commanding officer
DEROS	Date of estimated return from overseas
dink	A slang name used for Vietnamese
DMZ	Demilitarized Zone, separating South Vietnam from North Vietnam
ETS	End term of service
FAC	Forward Air Controller
FSB	Fire-support base
Go hot	Instruction from pilot to crew to fire weapons
gook	Slang name for the enemy
GS	General Support (people)
high ship	Helicopter high above landing zone reserved for rescue
hootch	A basic house or hut
IG	inspector general
KIA	Killed in action
LZ	Landing zone
MACV-SOG	Military Assistance Command Vietnam, Studies and Observation Group
MIA	Missing in action
M16	Army issue rifle
M60	Type of machine gun used on the Huey
NVA	North Vietnamese Army
OD	Officer of the Day
PZ	Pickup zone

POW	Prisoner of war
POL	Petroleum, oil, and lubricants
PX	Post Exchange
Rattler Six	Commanding officer's call sign of the 71st
R&R	Rest and relaxation
RPG	Rocket-propelled grenade
rpm	revolutions per minute
SAC	Senior Aircraft Commander
sapper	enemy demolition commando who crawls through perimeters to set explosive charges
SOP	Standard operating procedure
TPQ	Time position quadrants
UH1	Utility helicopter "Huey"
VC	Viet Cong
WIA	Wounded in action
WO	Warrant officer, a rank above enlisted men and below commissioned officers
WORWAC	Warrant Officer Rotary Wing Aviation Course
XO	Executive officer, second in command below the CO

BIBLIOGRAPHY

Aircraft of the World: The Complete Guide. Pittsburgh: IMP, 1997.

CNN.com. "'Blood and Fire' of My Lai Remembered 30 Years Later.' *CNN.com,* March 16, 1998. http://www.cnn.com/WORLD/9803/16/my.lai/.

Colvin, John. "The Tet Offensive 1968, General Vo Nguyen Giap." From *Vietnam Experience Nineteen Sixty-Eight,* Boston Publishing. Vets with a Mission. http://www.vwam.com/vets/tet/tet.html.

Davidson, Phillip B. *Vietnam at War.* Novato, CA: Presidio, 1988.

Forrest, Steve. "Tet Offensive: A Turning Point in the Vietnam War." *In Defense of Marxism.* http://www.marxist.com/1968/vietnam.html.

Fulbrook, Jim. "Lam Son 719, Part Two, the Battle." *U.S. Army Aviation Digest* (July 1986): 35–45.

________. "Lam Son 719, Part Three, Reflections and Values." *U.S. Army Aviation Digest* (August 1986): 2–13.

Fulghum, David and Terrence Maitland. *South Vietnam on Trial.* Boston: Boston Publishing, 1984.

Hersh, Seymour M. *Cover-Up.* New York: Random House, 1972.

Kimball, Jeffrey. *Nixon's Vietnam War.* Lawrence: University Press of Kansas, 1998.

Kissinger, Henry. *Ending the Vietnam War.* New York: Simon & Schuster, 2003.

Nixon, President Richard. "Vietnamization." Speech delivered November 3, 1969. Archived by the Program in Presidential Rhetoric, Dept. of Communications, Texas A&M University. http://www.tamu.edu/comm/pres/speeches/rmnvietnam.html.

Pike, Douglas M. *The Viet Cong Strategy of Terror.* Saigon: U.S. Mission Viet-Nam, 1970.

P.O.W. Network. "Bio, Becker James C." 1998. http://www.pownetwork.org/bios/b/b368.htm.

Roush, Gary. "Helicopter Losses during the Vietnam War." *The Vietnam Helicopter Pilots Association.* http://www.vhpa.org/heliloss.pdf.

Sloniker, Mike. "History of Lam Son 719." *Vietnam Helicopter Pilots Association 1994 Membership Directory,* vol. 11 (October 1994): 253–89.

Staggerwing.com. "Model Super E18S Specifications." http://www.staggerwing.com/tech_library/model_18_specs/specs_super_E18S.shtml.

Stubbe, Ray, ed. "A History of the Hill Battles of 1967." *Khe Sanh Veterans Newsletter, Special Issue: 30th Anniversary of the Hill Battles at Khe Sanh.* Khe Sanh Veterans Home Page. http:/www.geocities.com/Pentagon/4867/hillbatt.html.

Tucker, Spencer C. *Vietnam.* Lexington: University Press of Kentucky, 1999.

Vietnam Helicopter Flight Crew Network. "Statistics about the Vietnam War." http://vhfcn.org/stat.html. From Combat Area Casualty File, November 1993. Center for Electronic Records, National Archives, Washington, DC.

Vietnam Helicopter Pilots Association. "Cover Photo Analysis E." *Vietnam Helicopter Pilots Association* 1994 Membership Directory, vol. 11 (October 1994).

INDEX

B

C

K

L

M

W

Z